Must-See Websites

for Busy Teachers

Author

Lynn Van Gorp

Associate Editor
Peter Pulido

Assistant Editor
Katie Das

Editor-in-Chief
Sharon Coan, M.S.Ed.

Editorial Manager
Gisela Lee, M.A.

Creative Director
Lee Aucoin

Cover Design
Lesley Palmer

Interior Layout Designer
Don Tran

Print Production
Juan Chavolla
Phil Garcia

Publisher
Corinne Burton, M.A.Ed.

Learning Standards
Copyright 2004 McREL. www.mcrel.org/standards-benchmarks.

Trademarks
Trademarked names and websites appear throughout this book. Instead of listing every firm or entity that owns the trademarks or inserting a trademark symbol with each mention of a trademarked name or website, the publisher avers that it is using the names and websites only for editorial purposes and to the benefit of the trademarks' owners with no intention of infringing upon those trademarks.

Shell Education

5301 Oceanus Drive
Huntington Beach, CA 92649-1030

http://www.shelleducation.com
ISBN 978-1-4258-0474-9

© 2008 Shell Education

Table of Contents

Table of Contents *(cont.)*

Research

Research shows that the proper use of technology in education can benefit both students and teachers. Technology use is more commonplace now than it used to be, but its benefits still need to be emphasized. The following studies share relevant findings that reiterate that teachers should understand the importance of using technology and the Internet by themselves and with their students.

For teachers to use technology successfully in their classroom, several factors need to be in place. One is that teachers need to be comfortable with technology. Studies show that success happens when the training and experiences that are provided build interest and confidence. Abbott and Faris found that when teachers participated in a school-based practicum and literacy course, they were more likely to use technology in their classrooms than those who did not have the practicum. The course included writing technology-based lesson plans twice weekly, emailing others to share their ideas, and incorporating graphics in at least one assignment. The course was given by experienced teachers who mentored the teachers and modeled effective uses of technology (Abbott and Faris, 2000).

Teachers consistently report that they have inadequate time to learn to use new technologies. Teachers need to be sure to work with their administration to ensure they have a technology-based learning environment that is conducive to learning and using technology. In a review of studies on technology use, Cradler and Cradler found that staff development, training, and follow-up assistance are prerequisites for effective and sustained applications of technology. They reported that effective technology integration requires that technical assistance be available when needed; that adequate time to plan, learn about, and implement technology applications is required; that long-term staff development, rather than one-time workshops, is needed to support integration of technology into instruction; and that teachers need to have access to technology while planning (Cradler and Cradler, 1995).

Another factor that affects how much teachers use technology in the classroom is their technology use at home. Becker found that there was a correlation between teachers' home computer use and their professional use of technology in the classroom with students. His findings show that teachers with home Internet access felt more strongly about the need for using the Internet in their teachings and in their classrooms. They used the Internet twice as often as teachers who had Internet access somewhere in their school but not at home and not in their own classrooms (Becker, 1998).

Many studies show the positive impact technology use can have on students in the classroom. The studies show that it is important that the use of technology be relevant to the learning and that it is integrated into the curriculum. Bracewell and Laferriere's (1996) document review, *The Contribution of New Technologies to Learning and Teaching in Elementary and Secondary Schools*, shows that technology has the power to stimulate the development of intellectual skills such as reasoning and problem-solving ability, learning how to learn, and creativity.

Research (cont.)

In another review of studies, CEO Forum concluded that "technology can have the greatest impact when integrated into the curriculum to achieve clear, measurable educational objectives" (2001). Cradler and Cradler reported significant changes in student skills and knowledge after they completed their first multimedia project. They showed increased knowledge in research skills to locate content resources, capability to apply learning to real-world situations, organizational skills, and increased interest in the content (Cradler & Cradler, 1999).

Students can improve their critical thinking skills when they use technology as a tool to present, publish, and share results of their projects. The CAST study found that when students used the Internet to research topics, share information, and complete a final project within the context of a semi-structured lesson, they became independent critical thinkers (Coley, et al, 1997).

Teachers often worry about not having enough computers for each student to have his or her own computer when they work on research projects. Bracewell and Laferriere showed that when students worked together on one computer, the social interaction skills they developed through the teamwork were found to be more important than mastery of certain intellectual skills. The student at the keyboard provided more answers during discussions while the other student asked more questions (Bracewell and Laferriere, 1996).

Teachers should also think about encouraging their students' use of technology at home. Coley, et al, showed that higher-order thinking skills improve with home and school access to computers and the Internet. Students who were supplied with home computers and Internet access were compared with students who did not have this capability. Students with home computers and Internet access had an increase in all writing skills, better understanding and a broader view of math, greater problem-solving and critical thinking skills, an ability to teach others, greater self-confidence and self-esteem, and more confidence with computer skills.

Coley, et al, also showed that using computers and the Internet improves motivation, attitude, and interest, especially when it maximizes students' experience of success. Computer-based instruction can individualize instruction, provide instant feedback, and correct answers with explanations (Coley, et al, 1997).

Students show improved writing and spelling skills when they use technology. MacArthur showed that word processing was effective in helping students learn to revise and improve their writing when they consistently used word-processing software with a spell checker for their writing (MacArthur, 1995).

Technology has been found to increase learning when students use it to help plan and complete projects related to specific subjects (Bozeman, 1999). Bozeman showed that when students constructed computer simulation models to show what they learned in science, their learning was qualitatively greater than the learning shown with simple noncomputer-related classroom presentations.

This book provides teachers with resources for their own computer and Internet use, as well as resources that they can use to integrate technology into their curriculum and enhance their students' learning opportunities and environment.

Research [cont.]

You will find hundreds of websites in this book. They were handpicked for their content, design, and overall usefulness to a classroom or other educational environment. Some are lesson plans while others are multimedia resources. Many of these resources are for teachers while others are for their students.

Along with these new Internet resources comes a challenge for educators. Educators must keep up with the new technology: learn new computer applications, search a vast numbers of resources to make the classroom experience for students more real and valuable, and be able to select worthwhile sites. That is where this book can be helpful. The sites that have been chosen are some of the best that are available. This book will reduce the "looking for sites" time. Teachers can begin their search of sites with those contained in this book, thereby reducing their time spent online searching. People know that the Internet changes daily and that sites and links that existed today may not be found tomorrow. The sites chosen for this book are sites that are not as likely to change or disappear as quickly as other sites. They were selected from trusted sources that belong to government and educational institutions, organizations, agencies, museums, science centers, and companies in the business of education. For the most part, the sites that have been chosen do not belong to individuals who may have created great sites but might not be able to maintain them for long. When sites are not updated frequently and broken links are not fixed, users can become frustrated. The possibility of potential problem sites was kept to a minimum.

A significant area of concern by schools and teachers is safety on the Internet. Students and parents often need help in knowing how to choose safe Internet sites. Familiarize your students and their parents with Internet-safety information and make sure they understand how critical this information is to their safety and well-being. You will need to make sure that your equipment is protected and safe from viruses, and that your students are protected from inappropriate materials, advertising, and pop-ups. Make sure that your school has a firewall, virus protection, and blockers in place, and that they are functional. Make sure you protect your students. You will need permission from parents if you want to share class photos online. Make sure that if you do, you do not match student names with students in a photo and never give out your students' last names. If you allow your students to go on the Internet and participate in interactive projects, make sure they know not to share any personal information about themselves or their school. Teach them that they must not give out their last names, addresses, phone numbers, ages, or photos. Emphasize that they also need to know that they must never agree to meet someone in person that they have met and communicated with online.

Research *(cont.)*

You may want to take notes about the sites you visit. If you do not, you might get sites mixed up and not remember what each site has to offer. You may want to write in the margins of the page where the site is referenced, or you can create a database to record your site visits. If you take a file card approach, you can record specific information about each site. You might consider recording some of the following topics: Web Address, Curriculum Area, Grade Level, Standards Addressed, Summary of the Site's Content, Type of Resources Available, Student Use, Parent Use, General Comments, and Rating.

If you keep a record each time you visit or use a site, you will not find yourself unable to find a great site the second time around. With records, you will know what the site was and will be able to find it when you need it.

If you are fortunate enough to have easy access to classroom computers or a computer lab, think carefully about what you want your students to be doing while they are on the computers. There are so many informative, engaging, and creative sites and useful computer activities for students, but students need to be directed appropriately to make the best use of their time. Make sure you have a plan of what skills you, your school, and your district have deemed as necessary for your students to acquire, and make sure that you also enhance your students' learning with significant Internet resources and activities. You will love the benefits and so will your students. They will have more exposure to the world around them, and they will welcome the change in instructional methods from their usual classroom activities.

Shell Education (**http://www.shelleducation.com**) offers great resources. Look at the Research White Papers, Scientifically Based Research Reports, Critical Element Reviews, and Texas SBR that support the focus they take when creating their materials. All materials are standards based and many have won major awards. Resource materials are available for the following curriculum areas: Reading, Writing, Mathematics, Social Studies, Science, Technology, Test Preparation, and Professional Development. Sample pages are also available from their books and collections. Check out the resources they offer for free—Fun Fact Challenges, Free Activities, and Borders.

Prepare yourself for the future. Take computer training and learn more about the applications you are currently using. Do not have someone do these things for you. Ask them to help teach you how to do it independently. You may not think you are making progress because there is always someone around you that is doing more. Do not let that bother you. You are doing more now than when you first started using technology. That is progress. Be positive and realistic about what you can handle, and set small goals. You will make it, and your students will reap the benefits.

Introducing the Internet

What Is the Internet?

The Internet is an information resource comprised of a network of hundreds of millions of computers located throughout the world. It has changed the nature of research, global economics, the acquisition of information, and communications. There are two specific components of the Internet that are used in classrooms: the World Wide Web and electronic communications.

The World Wide Web, or Web, is a collection of interlinked documents called websites. Websites are created by governments, schools and colleges, businesses, nonprofit organizations, and individuals. Each website is a group of linked pages filled with text, graphics, audio files, animation, and other media. Users can browse the Internet for information, check world news, order airline tickets, buy almost any product, ask questions of various experts, chat with friends, or go on virtual trips around the world without ever leaving their computers. And, all of this can happen any time of the day or night.

In addition to websites, the Internet is also the network for electronic correspondence. Much of today's correspondence is done electronically through electronic mail, or email. Many adults and children successfully send and receive messages through the Internet using computers or other electronic devices. Digital video cameras (or webcams) can also be used to communicate in real time with others on the Web. The possibilities are endless.

Connecting to the Internet

In order to explore the Internet, you will need a minimum of the following things:

1. A computer that is capable of connecting to the Internet

2. Access to the Internet through a telephone line, cable network, digital subscriber line (DSL), wireless router, or a link to a server connected to the Internet

3. A browser (e.g. Internet Explorer, Mozilla Firefox, Netscape Navigator, Safari, and so on) or an Internet Service Provider (ISP), which is a commercial online service that offers Internet access through its own browser (America Online is an example of this.)

Most schools are connected to the Internet through a school or district-office server. This can provide a fast connection to the Internet so that teachers and students can enjoy an efficient service. In more remote areas, getting a connection may be slower and a bit more of a challenge to hook up. With more satellite service available, it is getting easier, but it is still not as simple or as cost effective as it can be in more populated areas with more available access.

Introducing the Internet [cont.]

Connecting to the Internet

A Web address, called a Uniform Resource Locator (URL), takes a user to a specified Web page. If you are entering it on the keyboard, it must be typed exactly as it appears in print or on the screen. Upper and lowercase letters; spaces; underscores (_), which sometimes look like spaces; slashes; periods; and special characters must all be typed correctly and carefully. Each part of the Web address has a particular purpose, and if it is not entered correctly, you will not get to the site you want.

Differentiation Using Computers

Computers are a great tool for differentiation in the classroom. Not everyone needs to complete the same assignments. You can assign different tasks at various ability levels. Students can work on different skills or do different projects at the same time. Also, in your classroom, students may need differing amounts of time to complete specific assignments. With flexible scheduling, you can easily provide each student sufficient time to finish the computer tasks you assign.

When you set up your computer schedules, it is not always a good idea to allow students to go to the computers when their assignments are finished. This can create an unbalanced use of the computers. If you always allow computer time for fast finishers, the students who need more time or are more thorough in their work cannot use the computers as often. To truly differentiate, make sure you allow all students in your class, no matter their abilities, fair use of the computers.

Take advantage of the multisensory capabilities of the computer and the Internet. There are great activities available online and many software titles available that will suit each student. Search online for appropriate sites and software.

Computers should not be used as time fillers. When planning computer-based activities, make sure the activity or task relates to what your students are studying or the skills you are teaching. You may want to start the year with all your students doing the same activities on the computer. This will make it easier to organize students and figure out how you are going to keep track of their progress. Once students get used to rotating through the computers as they would learning centers, you can start to differentiate their tasks. Pick two or three related tasks. Then, assign students to the tasks based on their academic needs, or allow students to choose from among the tasks based on their interests. For students who work more quickly, let them suggest their own computer tasks after they have completed those that you assigned.

Introducing the Internet [cont.]

Differentiation Using Computers [cont.]

It is important to coordinate the tasks you assign with the needs of the students. Students who have learning difficulties should be involved in tasks that provide immediate feedback and can be finished within the allotted time period. Successful completion of tasks is important. More advanced students should be offered open-ended tasks. These tasks can be more complicated and lengthy in nature.

Students love feedback. Have students print copies of their results or projects when they are finished. Students will find it rewarding to have copies of their finished products. A printout is also helpful for you to use in evaluating student progress.

Tips for Using the Internet

Safety Issues

Every school should have an administrator-approved Acceptable Use Policy (AUP) in place. Every year, this document should be signed by parents and students to acknowledge that they understand the laws, limitations to access, and responsibilities that are required for use of the school computers and the Internet. Your school's AUP should also make sure that everyone signing it understands the penalties and loss of privileges that will occur if the rules are broken.

It is absolutely essential for you and your students to be aware of the dangers that using the Internet can present. Provide your students with rules to follow when they are using the Internet, and be sure your students know the reasoning behind them, and their importance. (See pages 12–13 for suggested rules.)

It is also important for parents to know, understand, and reinforce your Internet rules. In fact, encourage parents to have rules at home that they require their children to follow. Internet service providers also have rules that must be followed. It is a good idea to know what these rules are so that you can share them with your students. If you are not familiar with the rules set up by your Internet Service Provider (ISP), contact them for more information.

Students should know what you and their parents expect them to do if they come across something inappropriate. A good procedure to use if something inappropriate comes up on a student's screen is to have the student turn off the monitor—not the computer—and get your or another adult's help. This method will allow you to check what came up on the screen. If the material should have been blocked, you can report the site to your administrator so your school's blocking software or controls can be checked. Stress to students that they should not make a fuss or draw attention to the site because you do not want other students to become involved. Make sure they understand that they do not need to be afraid to tell someone if an inappropriate site comes up because it can happen accidentally. Tell them that they need to report it to you because you can find out how they got to the site by looking at the computer's history. This way, you can prevent the problem from happening again. If students deliberately go to inappropriate sites, then you should be prepared with a consequence for this behavior.

Tips for Using the Internet *(cont.)*

Safety Issues *(cont.)*

If students are setting up email accounts through the school, it is very important that you set clear guidelines and consistently enforce them. When first setting up school email accounts, choose a specific pattern for your students' usernames and assign all students the same password. Many schools use a student's first name and surname initial (lynnm). Also, have your controls set so you can access a student's school-sponsored account at any time. You may want to let them change their passwords once you set up the accounts so other students cannot get into their accounts, but make sure that you can override their password so you can still monitor their accounts if there is a problem. Students should know they can set up personal email accounts at home, but that their school accounts will not be kept private if there is a problem within their accounts.

If students receive inappropriate email sent from another student, make sure students know that they should not delete the email. Have them show you the email, and then if action needs to be taken, print a copy of the email. Be sure to include the From, To, and Date information as well as the body of the email. Deal with the student who sent the email in a way that will let students know that bullying and rude or inappropriate emails are unacceptable.

Student Guidelines for Safe Surfing

These are some simple rules to set up for your students' use of the Internet at school. Feel free to use these rules or write your own.

1. Only go to the sites for which you have permission. Ask your teacher if you're unsure.

2. Use only the search engines that are approved for your use. Use proper search techniques and search for appropriate material only.

3. Never guess a website address or email address. You might end up at an inappropriate site or communicate with someone you should not be contacting.

4. Never give out personal information such as your name, address, phone numbers, passwords, or age. It is also extremely important to avoid giving information about your parents or credit cards.

5. Never send a personal photograph to someone or use one on a website without permission from your teacher.

Student Guidelines for Safe Surfing [cont.]

6. Never agree to meet or get together with anyone you have met online without your parents' permission and without an adult going with you. This is one of the most dangerous things you can do. Remember, the person you meet in a chat room or through email may not be the person you think you have met. Unfortunately, some people use the Internet to harm children and young adults.

7. Never send an inappropriate or threatening email. Remember, your email can be forwarded and viewed by others. Always think about whether you would like your parents or principal to see what you have sent. If not, do not send it.

8. Tell your teacher or parents if anyone sends you an inappropriate, rude, or threatening email.

9. Respect and follow these rules. They are in place to help you enjoy your time online and be safe.

Netiquette or Online Politeness

It is very important that Internet users have a good understanding of acceptable, polite online behavior. Being online is like being at the dinner table or in school, church, or someone else's home. It requires the use of appropriate manners. While there are no Internet police to serve and protect individuals from rude or unruly users, there is a code of behavior called Netiquette that is implied, and can be enforced by Internet service providers, teachers, or parents. Unacceptable behavior can result in lost privileges or cancellation of a family's services.

Use Your Netiquette—Be Polite Online

The following guidelines can be shared with your students:

1. Follow the golden rule: Do unto others, as you would have them do unto you. Be nice!

2. Never use the computer to harm anyone. Do not use bad words or say unkind things to others.

3. Do not think that everyone is interested in everything you have to send. Never send meaningless emails, and do not forward junk mail or chain letters. Forwarding an email you enjoyed to everyone at school not only clogs up the school's email system, but also many students may not be interested in what you send. Friends will pay more attention to what you send if you are thoughtful about your emails. They will value receiving an email from you.

Tips for Using the Internet *[cont.]*

Use Your Netiquette—Be Polite Online *[cont.]*

4. Be careful what you write and share online. Keep the content appropriate and be sure to check your grammar and spelling. Even though others do not seem to care, and you may think it does not matter, do not get in the habit of being careless and sloppy. You will find that your overall writing skills will decline if you do not use the best skills you have. Be proud of what you send.

5. Respect boundaries. Never go into anyone else's files. Do not use anyone else's email or website memberships. Never let anyone access your email account or any of your Web memberships.

6. Be sure to pay for materials or sites that require a fee, and do not give the materials to others unless you have the right to do so. Do not cheat anyone.

7. Protect all your private information such as User IDs or passwords. If you choose to share, do not be surprised if problems occur.

8. Lurk before you leap! Take the time to explore or watch what is happening in a chat room or on a discussion board before you participate. Make sure it is appropriate and that your identity is protected. Get off the site if you find that people are using inappropriate words or are discussing inappropriate topics.

9. Do not copy or plagiarize materials. Give credit where credit is due.

10. Use your computer time wisely. Enjoy the great interactive sites; do not waste your time online with foolish or rude sites.

11. Report problems you have with sites. This will not only help you, but it will help control the Internet environment and make it a more pleasant place to be.

12. Look for good role models and model their behaviors. Be a good role model for other students and your family members.

Security on the Internet

Internet users must be aware of the need for safety and security on the Internet. While some things will be handled at your school or district office, remember that students may be transferring or downloading content to your computers. It is your responsibility to make sure that your students follow your Internet rules and stay safe online. You do not want infected files to ruin documents, files, or computer systems.

Viruses on the Internet

Computer viruses can seriously damage your computer. A virus can enter your computer through the Internet from something that is downloaded or opened from email or email attachments. Someone can transfer bad or virus-infected files or data to your computer from a CD, DVD, or flash drive as well. One of the best ways to protect your computer(s) is to use an antivirus software application. School districts and individual schools are usually well protected. Do not assume this is the case, though. Check to see what is in place at your school. Make sure your students' parents are aware of the importance of good protection, too.

Tips for Using the Internet (cont.)

Viruses on the Internet (cont.)

While most Internet Service Providers supply great protective software because they do not want any of the computers using their system to have problems, not all service providers do. Make sure your students and their parents check to see what protection they have for their computers at home. If they do not have any protection, you might suggest they use one of the more popular applications, like McAfee's or Norton's virus scan software.

Once a computer has antivirus software installed, the software needs to be on and scanning each time the computer is turned on and when anything is downloaded. The software also needs to be updated regularly and subscriptions may need to be annually renewed. You need to have your computer check the Internet for updates and download them. Companies like McAfee or Norton constantly update their software to catch and fix current problems. Not having your software updated constantly and not having it scan regularly can make your virus software useless.

Adware Software

One of the more bothersome problems online today is all the advertising and pop-ups that appear. Not only is this annoying, but these companies can download tracking software and dialers to your computer that can slow down your computer significantly or do damage to it. If you have a service that will block pop-ups and SPAM (unwanted email and advertising), make sure you have it turned on. If not, you may want to download software that will do this for you. A popular software application to use for pop-ups and advertising is called Ad-Aware SE Personal Edition by Lavasoft. This software application can be downloaded for free. It will work best if it is run often, particularly if you find your computer is slowing down.

Shopping, Security, and Spyware

Another fear of Internet users is whether or not personal details such as credit card numbers will be kept confidential. If a site has encryption technology, which uses a code-scrambling system, there should be no problem. If you are uncomfortable, ask for alternative ways of providing information or payment. Another suggestion is to have one credit card that you only use online. That way, if a security breach happens, it will only affect that particular account, and you can easily keep track of your online purchases.

Tips for Using the Internet [cont.]

Setting Parent Controls or Content Advisors

Check to see what controls are being used on your computers to protect your students. Some controls such as monitoring inappropriate language and the control of inappropriate images and sites should be in place. Make sure your students' parents know how to check what protection is provided by their Internet Service Providers. Many services offer parental controls for email, instant messaging, online time, and chatting. Controls can also be set differently for different age groups such as kids under 12, young teens, and mature teens.

Communicating with Parents

It is a good idea to talk to parents about your computer education program. Back-to-school night is always a good forum, but since not all parents come to that event, it is also a good idea to send home a technology packet. The packet should have a letter to the parents that they need to sign and return. This way, parents will have been informed of your plans and your rules, and you will be protected. Parents also need to sign your school's Acceptable Use Policy document each year. An AUP is not specific to your class computer program packet; your packet will allow you to communicate with your parents directly.

Your packet to parents should include a letter that explains what it is you will be doing with their children and outlines the types of general computer activities and Internet tasks you have planned. Explain why you feel that using the computer and the Internet are valuable uses of each student's time. If you want, you can use the ideas shared on page 6–8. Share your specific goals too. You should also explain how you plan to differentiate the use of the computers. Many parents still believe that using the computer is playtime and that it takes away from basic instruction. This is an important myth to dispel.

Tell parents of the need for them to have virus, adware, and spyware protection on their home computers. Make sure they also understand the importance of keeping that software up to date. Have them check the options their ISP has for safety and security. You can also discuss the types of safety controls you have in place at school and in your classroom. Tell them what type of material is blocked and the procedures you have in place when something inappropriate comes up on a student's screen.

Also, tell them that they can use the parental control option provided by their ISP to put some limits on the Internet access their children have at home. Most parents want inappropriate language and images controlled. With the problems that have been occurring at sites like MySpace, parents may want to restrict their children's use of email, chat rooms, and personal Web page sites.

Communicating with Parents [cont.]

Finally, provide parents with a list of grade-appropriate sites that they may want to use with their children and that their children can use for homework. Review the sites presented in this book and select the ones that best suit your students. If you have the time, you can even personalize the list, giving parents specific sites that will help with their children's particular learning needs.

The packet should include a copy of your school's AUP for them to keep as well as a copy of your classroom computer and Internet rules. Make sure the parents understand that they need to read all the documents, review them with their children, sign the letter, and return the letter to you. (If you are collecting the AUP at this time, send home two copies. They can sign and return one and keep the other for reference.) Stress that once their child's letter has been returned, he or she will have computer privileges.

Copyright Guidelines

As Internet use grows, so do the instances of plagiarism in today's classrooms. Not every student means to plagiarize when he or she does not cite an Internet source. Sometimes, students do not realize the need to cite their sources, or they do not know how to best cite their references. It is important to teach students why they need to cite all Internet and print resources and how you expect them to do it. Modeling proper reference citations in your own work is one of the best ways to teach students this important skill.

When someone invests time and effort in a website and students use the work, it is only right to give that person credit. Students need to be taught that it is plagiarism if they do not give credit when and where credit is due. Without credit, the work will appear to be their own, and that is considered theft of intellectual property.

Teach students that they can make limited use of someone's work providing they give proper credit and they do not profit from its use. It's important for them to keep in mind that the person who wrote the material they are using is the true owner of that material. They are just borrowing it to support their work. It is best if you teach students to send an email to the website asking permission to use the material, particularly if the material is going to be shown to many people beyond the individual's own classroom.

In today's technologically advanced world, almost everything is copyrighted the minute it is written on the Internet. No copyright note is required. Written articles, research material, lesson plans, email, and material posted in newsgroups or on bulletin boards are copyrighted. And, students and teachers should not assume that by using an author's material they are helping to promote original work. The author may appreciate it, but he or she will appreciate it more if you ask permission and give credit. In some cases, the author may have a valid reason for not granting people permission to use the work.

Tips for Using the Internet [cont.]

Copyright Guidelines [cont.]

Educators often use what is called *fair use*. This does not mean that anything can be used at any time. But it does mean that students and teachers can use materials for educational purposes within their classrooms. However, students should still be encouraged to use their own words and keep what is directly quoted to a minimum. Students also need to give credit to the original author of any work that is referenced or quoted. Students and teachers often use photographs, graphic images, or streaming video from websites. These, too, need to be acknowledged.

Citing Internet Sources

It is important to collect the right information about sources when conducting Internet research. Every website students visit should be recorded in their notes. The citations should include the author's last and first name (if available); the title of the article, image, audio, or video clip; the website address (URL); and the date the document was created on the website, or if that is not available, the date the site was visited.

Next, you need to select a style for citing your resources. Create a document with a few examples of different types of resources and give it to your students to reference. Here are two examples:

- Brians, Paul. *Common Errors in English Usage.*
  http://www.wsu.edu/~brians/errors/index.html, (accessed May 31, 2007).
- Teacher Created Materials. Free Activities for Teachers.
  http://www.teachercreatedmaterials.com/free, (accessed May 31, 2007).

How do I Search the Internet?

In November 2006, the Educational Testing Service reported that out of 6,300 high school and college students only 40 percent knew how to use multiple terms in a Web search to narrow the results (Trotter 2007). This information shows how important it is to teach your students how to conduct advanced searches. Success comes with understanding how search engines work and how to begin a search.

How Do I Search the Internet? *[cont.]*

Types of Search Engines

Keyword Search

A keyword search engine looks for the word or words you have entered and returns a list of sites that match your entry. One of the most popular keyword search engines is Google (**http://www.google.com**). If you were looking for information on inventing the telephone for example, you could enter the words "inventing the telephone" as search words. Include the quotation marks because that helps to narrow the search. For this example, Google returned 940,000 entries. The entries listed at the top of the list are often the most relevant, but watch out for sponsored sites that paid for locations on the top of the screen. One would generally use this type of search when you know exactly what you want to find out. The keyword choice helps to quickly narrow your search and can focus on the results quickly. Google lets you search for images with keywords, too. Google Image Search can be found at **http://images.google.com/**.

Google is a good search engine to use at school because inappropriate sites can be blocked. Under **Preferences**, one can select *Safe Search Filtering*, and then select *Use Strict Filtering (Filter both explicit text and explicit images)*. Google's Safe Search blocks Web pages containing explicit sexual content from appearing in the search results.

Directory Search

In a directory search, information is organized into different categories. You usually begin by selecting a broad category and a subcategory, and then you finish with a specific topic. For example, you may be looking for information on Cinco de Mayo. First, you might start with the broad category, by typing "Around the World." Next, you might select the subcategory "Holiday," and finish with finding the topic in which you were interested, "Cinco de Mayo." When you use a directory as a search engine, you go through the process of refining your search as you go along until you come to a group of sites that relate to your topic. With this type of search, you may not have something specific in mind when you start; you may just have a broad topic in mind and refine it as you go along. A great example of a directory search engine for students in elementary and middle schools is Yahoo! Kids. It can be found at **http://kids.yahoo.com/reference/index**. It is part of the adult directory search engine Yahoo! at **http://www.yahoo.com/**. While directory search engines tend to focus on categories, they usually also have a keyword search engine as part of their sites.

How Do I Search the Internet? [cont.]

Types of Search Engines [cont.]

Metasearch Engine

To make several search engines work for you at the same time, you can use a metasearch engine. A metasearch engine will return combined results from several search engines all at the same time. Metacrawler is a popular metasearch engine. It can be found at **http://www.metacrawler.com**. Another popular metasearch engine, especially with students, is Dogpile. It can be found at **http://www.dogpile.com/**.

Search Tips

Each search engine has a Help section. Be sure to visit that section to get a better understanding of the functions and features of the search engine. If you follow the tips and suggestions provided, you will have a more efficient and effective search experience.

To decide on appropriate keywords for a keyword search, you will need to do several things. While you may not need to write them down, you should:

- Define your topic: What is it you need to know or research? How much information do you have on your topic? Do you need more clarification?

- Identify your search goal: Are you going to be writing a research paper or making a slide show? What would you like your search to provide for you—information, facts, quotes, photographs, charts, or data?

- Decide if the type of information you need is general or specific. Do you need to know general concepts, or do you need to know specific details, events, people, or places?

- Define relevant keywords. Make your keywords as specific as possible. Do not use terms that are hard to define, like *economics* or *politics*. For example, "economics of World War II" or "politics of World War II" is very general. Instead, you might try "women working during World War II."

- Decide which keywords are the most important and list them first. With the example of "women working during World War II," you would put your keywords in that order since you are primarily interested in information about women working during World War II.

How Do I Search the Internet?

Search Tips *[cont.]*

- You do not need to use little words as part of your keyword selection. You would not need to use "during" from the example "women working during World War II."

- Most search engines are not case sensitive. That means that they do not recognize capital letters. "Martin Luther King Jr." would be considered the same as "martin luther king jr."

- If you want to be more specific with your searches, use Boolean operators. Simply add the words *and*, *or*, and *not* to better focus your search. For example, you might use "World War II Politicians" and "Winston Churchill" as your search words. The search engine looks for documents containing the words *World War II politicians* and *Winston Churchill*. If you use "World War II politicians" or "Winston Churchill," the search engine looks for documents that include the words *World War II politicians* and looks separately for documents containing the words *Winston Churchill*. If you use "World War II politicians" not "Winston Churchill," the search engine looks for documents that contain the words *World War II politicians*. It would not select any documents that contain the words *Winston Churchill*.

- Sometimes the words you select will not provide any results. If that happens, you need to think of other ways to describe what it is you need. Perhaps your words are too general, or you used a phrase that was too specific, or maybe you should try using a directory search engine before you use a keyword search. Searching requires you to follow the saying, "If at first you do not succeed, try, try again."

What You Need to Successfully Use the Internet

Plug-ins and Active X Controls

Sometimes your computer needs add-on software that gives your Internet browser the ability to do extra things when you are viewing a website. These include playing music, displaying animation, or showing videos. Some of these come with your computer, while others can be downloaded as you need them. Most are free or inexpensive.

Some of the common plug-ins and Active X controls you will need for the activities and games you use include:

- *Windows Media Player*—plays many different sound and video files

- *Shockwave*—used for interactive games, multimedia, video clips, graphics, and streaming video

What You Need to Successfully Use the Internet [cont.]

Plug-ins and Active X Controls [cont.]

- *QuickTime*—used as a virtual reality viewer

- *RealPlayer*—plays streaming audio, video, animations, and multimedia presentations on the Web; plays popular media file types like MP3

- *MacroMedia Flash Player*—plays animation

A Strong Web Browser

A browser is the program that you use to navigate the World Wide Web—to go to websites and Web pages. Some of the most popular Web browsers are Internet Explorer, Mozilla Firefox, Netscape Navigator, and Safari for Macs.

Most browsers operate in much the same way. Browsers have address boxes at the top of the screen. This is where the Web address is displayed for the current site, or where you can enter an address if you want to go somewhere different. The area below the address box is where the Web page is viewed.

The best thing about most Web browsers is that they can be personalized. You can add a connection to your Web-based email service or add links to places of interest to you and your students. For example, if you want to check the weather every day, you may want a link to the weather channel; if you want your students to check the news, you may want to add a news channel link. By providing a display of information or quick access to it, you can save valuable time in your classroom.

Make sure you use the Favorites or Bookmarks feature of your browser to your advantage, too. This is the spot where students can find addresses quickly and accurately. It can save time, and students will be less likely to make errors typing in Web addresses.

The History button on your Web browser will let you see what sites have been visited. You can set this to keep as many sites as you want in its memory. It is a good idea to check this option periodically to make sure your students are not going to sites that you do not allow. Letting your students know you can check where they have been is often a good deterrent for misuse.

#50475—*Must-See Websites for Busy Teachers*

What You Need to Successfully Use the Internet (cont.)

A Strong Web Browser (cont.)

As you go from site to site, you will find that there will be times when you are unable to reach a site. You may have typed in the Web address incorrectly, or the Web address may have changed. Check your address or follow the suggestions your Web browser provides. Sometimes, sites have changed their addresses or no longer exist. If this is the case, change your Bookmarks or Favorites list. Sometimes an inappropriate site will take a good site's place, so you need to be vigilant.

Key Technology Skills

Printing Material Found on a Web Page

When you are surfing the Internet and you find something you want to keep, your instinct may be to hit the Print button. This is not always the best decision. Since Web pages are not always a standard size and do not stop at what you see on the screen, you could be printing a lot of extra material—graphics, links, and other advertising material that you do not want. A Web page can be wider than a standard 8 x 11 inch paper, so some of the material might be cut off. Both of these circumstances would result in a waste of paper and ink.

To remedy this, you can highlight only the material you want and print that material. Or better yet, you can highlight what you want to print, and then copy and paste it into a word processing document. The document can then be saved and printed when all the material that is required has been gathered. Also, keep your eyes out for a Print View icon on the website. Sometimes Web designers have set up a way to easily print your materials.

References Cited

Abbott, J. A., Faris, S. E. (2000). Integrating technology into pre-service literacy instruction: A survey of elementary education students' attitudes toward computers. *Journal of Research on Computing in Education, 33*(2), 149–161.

Becker, H. J. (1998). *Internet use by teachers* (Report No. 1). Irvine, CA: Teaching, Learning, & Computing.

Bozeman W. C. (1999). *Educational technology: Best practices from America's schools.* Larchmont, NY: Eye on Education, Inc. pp. 233–240.

Bracewell, R., and Laferriere, T. (1996). *The contribution of new technologies to learning and teaching in elementary and secondary schools* (Document review). http://www.fse.ulaval.ca/fac/tact/fr/html/apport/impact96.html

CEO Forum on Education and Technology. (2001, June). *The CEO Forum school technology and readiness report: Key building blocks for student achievement in the 21st century.* http://www.ceoforum.org/downloads/report4.pdf.

Coley, R., Cradler, J. and Engel, P. (1997). *Computers and classrooms: The status of technology in U.S. schools.* Princeton, NJ: Educational Testing Service, Policy Information Center, 37.

Cradler, J., and Cradler, R. (1995). *Prior studies for technology insertion.* San Francisco, CA: Far West Laboratory.

Cradler, R., & Cradler, J. (1999). *Just in time: Technology innovation challenge grant year 2 evaluation report for Blackfoot School District No. 55.* San Mateo, CA: Educational Support Systems.

MacArthur, C. A., Graham, S., Schwartz, S. S., and Schafer, W. D. (1995). Evaluation of a writing instruction model that integrated a process approach, strategy instruction, and word processing. *Learning Disability Quarterly, 18,* 278–291.

How to Use This Book

This book was written to give classroom teachers access to online resources for education, technology, professional organizations and lessons in all subject matters to use in the classrooms with their kindergarten through 12th-grade students. The Web can be a little overwhelming and confusing. By using the resources in this book, you will find an orderly way to look at your subject areas and decide which lessons or Internet resources will benefit your students. A CD-ROM is provided at the back of the book with active links to make it easier for you to access the websites. Just find and click on the hyperlink and you will be directed to the website through your Internet browser. Always look at each website before you use it with your students or suggest it for home use. You will want to be sure that it fits the needs of your students and parents, and you certainly do not want any surprises while browsing in class with your students or while parents are working with their children at home. Every attempt was made to include only the best and most reliable sites in this book. However, be aware that over time some websites can change or become unavailable for use. Sometimes when this happens, you will automatically be redirected to the new site address. If not, check the main address or the home page of the website on which the Web page was hosted. Often when you do that, you will be given other worthwhile Web page selections.

Website Resource Lists

The listings of resources are grouped by the following topics:

- Art and Music Resources
- Classroom Management
- Communicating Online
- Early Childhood Resources
- Education Laws and Standards
- Foundations and Grant-Providing Organizations
- Government Resources
- Health and Physical Education Resources
- Holiday Resources
- Lesson Plans and Teacher Resources
- Language Arts and Literature Resources
- Math Resources
- Professional Teacher Organizations
- Science Resources
- Searching the Web
- Social Studies
- Special Education
- Teacher and Students Online Reference Sites
- Technology Resources
- Test Practice and Homework Help

Each website listing includes the website's title, URL address, and an annotation that briefly describes the website.

Correlations to Standards

The No Child Left Behind (NCLB) legislation mandates that all states adopt academic standards that identify the skills children will learn in kindergarten through grade 12. While many states had already adopted academic standards prior to NCLB, the legislation set requirements to ensure the standards were detailed and comprehensive. Standards are designed to focus instruction and guide adoption of curricula. Standards are statements that describe the criteria necessary for children to meet specific academic goals. They define the knowledge, skills, and content children should acquire at each level. Standards are also used to develop standardized tests to evaluate children' academic progress. In many states today, teachers are required to demonstrate how their lessons meet state standards. State standards are used in the development of Shell Education products, so educators can be assured that this product meets strict federal academic requirements.

How to Find Your State Correlations

Shell Education is committed to producing educational materials that are research and standards based. In this effort, all products are correlated to the academic standards of the 50 states, the District of Columbia, and the Department of Defense Dependent Schools. A correlation report customized for your state can be printed directly from the Shell Education website: **http://www.shelleducation.com**. If you require assistance in printing correlation reports, please contact Customer Service at 1-800-877-3450.

McREL Compendium

Shell Education uses the Mid-continent Research for Education and Learning (McREL) Compendium to create standards correlations. Each year, McREL analyzes state standards and revises the compendium. By following this procedure, they are able to produce a general compilation of national standards. Each sample lesson in this book is based on one or more McREL content standards. This chart shows the McREL standards that correlate to each lesson used in the book.

Grades	Technology Standard
1–8	Knows the characteristics and uses of computer hardware and operating systems.
1–8	Understands the nature and uses of different forms of technology.
6–8	Uses Boolean searches to execute complex searches.

Art and Music Resources

Introduction

The sites in this section cover art and music. Children can learn about art and music and think, create, and have fun at the same time. Both younger and older children will benefit from these great sites.

All the art websites provided have activities and games that allow students to explore independently and to complete interactive art projects online. Students can also learn about art from all over the world, famous artists, and art periods by exploring these websites. Lesson plans are also available for teachers who need art-related resources for their classroom. The most famous art galleries have websites that students can explore through online virtual tours and tutorials.

Get your students engaged in learning music principles as well as experimenting with music. The sites presented by well-known philharmonic orchestras are incredibly rich in their offerings and should not be missed.

Also included are photography sites. Many classrooms now use digital still and video cameras. It is important for students to learn how to take great photographs and movies and creatively present them.

SUGGESTED activity

Visit Sandford's A Lifetime of Color—Art Adventures and Art Education Resources at **http://www.sanford-artedventures.com/**. Here you will find lesson plans for grades K–8. Study the lesson plans and find which ones work for your particular class. Let your students have fun and create their own art with the Create Art section. When your students have the time and access to the Internet, allow them to go to the Study Art section to research art principles, styles, media, artists, and other art concepts. They can also go to the Play Art Games section and explore the different options available for fun and enjoyment.

Art and Music Resources (cont.)

Art Activities and Games

Inside Art: An Art History Game

http://www.eduweb.com/insideart/index.html

These are Educational Web Adventures' first art-history adventures. Kids will love being taken on an adventure and will learn art history. There are teacher resources provided, too.

Enchanted Learning—Art, Artists, and Art Activities and Projects for Students

http://www.enchantedlearning.com/artists/projects.shtml

Teachers of younger children love this site. Students can explore the site independently. It has a section on art and artists, and another on art activities and projects for students. The selections include graphics that make it easy to navigate. This site is very student- and parent-friendly.

Kinderart—Art Projects for Kids

http://www.kinderart.com

The lesson plans and activities provided at this site are extensive, interesting, and creative. Some of the sections include Art History, Architecture, Cross-Curricular Art, Drawing, Multicultural Art, Painting, Print Making, Sculpture, Folk Art, Textiles, Kinder Kitchen, Kids Art Gallery, Contests for Kids, and Stuff for Teachers.

Wacky Kids

http://www.wackykids.org/

This is a fascinating website for kids from the Denver Art Museum. Its creative art projects will keep students busy for hours. Kids can explore art from around the world. This site is geared to the lower elementary-level student.

NGA Kids—An Interactive Art Project

http://www.nga.gov/kids/

The National Gallery of Art has great art-related activities for students. They will love the artist-related games and the interactive art they can create. Some of the project titles include Collage Machine, Moble, Pixel Face, 3-D Twirler, Cubits, Diamonds, River Run, Paintbox, Wallovers, Swatch Box, Flow, and Jungle. This is an exciting site to visit.

Art Activities and Games [cont.]

A. Pintura: Art Detective

http://www.eduweb.com/pintura/

A. Pintura: Art Detective is an online game about art history and art composition. In the game, students play a 1940s detective with a degree in art history. An upset woman wants them to help identify the artist who made a painting she found in her grandfather's attic. Participants must examine paintings by famous artists, looking at composition, style, and subject. This game captures children's attention right up to the end, where a twist reveals the woman's identity and her motives. There are also links to new games such as The Artist's Toolkit: Visual Elements and Principles, A Brush with Wildlife: Create a Composition with Carl Rungius, Sanford's A Lifetime of Color, Art Edventures, and Art Education Resources.

Incredible Art Department—Links to Art for Kids

http://www.princetonol.com/groups/iad/links/artgames.html

This site takes time to explore, but there are great resources to be found that might be appropriate to add to your art curriculum. There are links to art activities and games, art groups, art periods and styles, and art zines. It is worth the time to look.

Art Safari

http://www.moma.org/momalearning/artsafari/safari_menu.html

People love safaris. Do you want to encourage your students to write more? In Art Safari, students explore animals and pieces of art by Pablo Picasso, Frida Kahlo, Henri Rousseau, and Diego Rivera. Then, they are asked a series of questions to help them write stories based on the different artworks. The questions ask them to describe what they see and help develop their observational skills. Students can have fun and write more easily when they are guided and follow a structure. When they finish, be sure your students share their stories. Ask them what they liked about these incredible artists too.

Smart Kids from the Smart Museum of Art, University of Chicago

http://smartmuseum.uchicago.edu/smartkids/index.html

This site is designed for students ages 7–12 to interactively discover ways to look at, study, think about, and respond creatively to art. It has four major sections—Look and Share, Art Detective, Art Speak, and Artist Studio.

Art and Music Resources [cont.]

Art Lesson Plans Sites

Incredible Art Department—Just for Kids—Art Education Links

http://www.princetonol.com/groups/iad/lessons/middle/for-kids.htm

This site has everything: extensive listings for art history, art museums, art techniques, art projects, and using art to learn about cultures. There are also curriculum resources for use in art lesson planning.

Arts Edge: Linking Art and Education through Technology

http://artsedge.kennedy-center.org/

This site is sponsored by the Kennedy Center for K–12 teachers and students. It includes lessons, standards, and Web links. It also has a Today in Art section, a Meet the Artist section, and Look-Listen-and-Learn activities.

Sanford's A Lifetime of Color—Art Adventures and Art Education Resources

http://www.sanford-artedventures.com/

Teachers and students can select Create Art, Study Art, Play Art Games, or Teach Art. There are extensive resources for each section that are suitable for a variety of ages and experiences.

Art Links Archives

http://www.arts.ufl.edu/art/rt_room/archives/link-archives.html

The art links at this comprehensive site have been organized into 10 categories. The categories include Artists, Art Museums, World Art, Special Exhibits, Fun On-Line, Art Study, Kids Art, By Kids, Odds and Ends, and WebQuests.

Art History Resources on the Web

http://witcombe.bcpw.sbc.edu/ARTHLinks.html

Christopher Witcombe, a professor of art history at Sweet Briar College, Virginia, created this site. It has been on the web for 11 years and is updated regularly. Its collection of links to sites is extensive and includes art history from many cultures and time periods.

Art and Music Resources (cont.)

Artists

Exploring Leonardo—Scientist, Inventor, Artist

http://www.mos.org/leonardo/index.html

This Museum of Science site offers resources for learning about Leonardo da Vinci. It includes lesson plans for grades 4–8 and classroom activities, along with a multimedia zone.

PBS—The Life and Times of Frida Kahlo

http://www.pbs.org/weta/fridakahlo/

At this site, students can explore the symbolism and meaning in five of Frida Kahlo's famous works at this PBS interactive site. They can discover the connection between each painting and Kahlo's own life.

Welcome to Claude Monet's Giverny

http://giverny.org/monet/welcome.htm

This site allows students to visit Monet's house and gardens where he loved to paint. They can also review a biography of Monet, look at copies of his paintings, study the colors he used, and check out current exhibitions of his art.

Pablo Picasso

http://www.picasso.fr/anglais/

This unique site offers links to images of Picasso's work, information about his life, and museums that show his art.

Art and Music

Art and Music Resources [cont.]

Galleries

National Gallery of Art—Washington, D.C. Online Tour

http://www.nga.gov/onlinetours/index.shtm

Students can choose an online tour by art school or medium to explore the National Gallery's collections of painting, sculpture, works on paper, photographs, and decorative arts. They can also explore a specific artist, work of art, or theme.

National Gallery of London—Online Collection

http://www.nationalgallery.org.uk/collection/default.htm

The National Gallery of London has Gallery Features, Beginner's Guides, Collections at a Glance, Artists at a Glance, Collection Explorer, and an Education Option with Teacher Resources.

Smithsonian Museum—Art and Design

http://www.si.edu/art_and_design/

Art and Design is one of three sections at the Smithsonian Museum's website. This section does an excellent job of presenting highlights of art and culture with choices of different regions and cultures.

The Louvre—Paris

http://www.louvre.fr/llv/commun/home_flash.jsp?bmLocale=en

This official site for the Louvre has wonderful photographs showing the outside and inside of the gallery. Check out their visual tours. Their Close-Up feature allows students to explore famous paintings at close range. The Mona Lisa painting is part of this Close-Up option.

Destination Modern Art—Museum of Modern Art—New York City

http://www.moma.org/destination/

This is a delightful comic animation designed to introduce young students to modern art. It uses a space alien cartoon to explore the museum that captures students' attention well.

Art and Music Resources (cont.)

Galleries (cont.)

The Getty Museum of Art—Los Angeles

http://www.getty.edu/museum/

Younger students will enjoy the games section. The games introduce students to art and help them become familiar with famous works.

Van Gogh Museum—Amsterdam, Holland

http://www3.vangoghmuseum.nl/vgm/index.jsp

The opening screen's dramatic images of Van Gogh's work will capture anyone's interest. The multimedia presentation, Van Gogh—An Overview, is definitely the best place to start. Students will find it offers an interesting perspective on his life.

History of Music

Internet Public Library—History of Music

http://www.ipl.org/div/mushist/

This is a guide to western composers and their music from the middle ages to the present.

Music Activities and Games

The Music Room

http://www.empire.k12.ca.us/capistrano/Mike/capmusic/music_room/themusic.htm

Michael Bower has created an excellent resource for teaching music. It is comprehensive and a great way to decide what you might want to focus on in your music program.

New York Philharmonic for Kids

http://www.nyphilkids.org

This site has a game room, a composer's gallery where students can learn about different composers, an instrument lab where they can make their own instrument, an instrument storage room where they can learn about different instruments, and a musicians' lounge where they can meet the different musicians of the New York Philharmonic.

Art and Music Resources [cont.]

Music Activities and Games [cont.]

San Francisco Symphony for Kids

http://www.sfskids.org

This site provides a great way for students to hear, learn, and have fun with music. It has a Music Lab section where students can learn about music composition and experiment with the sights and sounds of music.

Dallas Symphony for Kids

http://www.dsokids.com/

At this site, students can hear any instrument of the orchestra, play games, listen to major and minor scales, and access information on composers with attached audio files.

National Arts Center of Canada—Arts Alive—Music

http://www.artsalive.ca/en/mus/index.asp

At the National Art Center of Canada, students can learn all about orchestral music, great composers, conductors, and the NAC Orchestra and its musicians and friends.

Creating Music

http://www.creatingmusic.com/

Creating Music is a creative music environment. Children can compose music using a musical sketchpad or a rhythm band tool, play musical games, and solve music puzzles.

Art and Music Resources [cont.]

Music Lesson Plan Sites

Lesson Plans Page—Music

http://www.lessonplanspage.com/Music.htm

Great ideas for lessons in music are available at this site. Teachers can select by grade level for easy navigation.

Teachnology—Teacher's Lesson Plans for Music

http://www.teach-nology.com/teachers/lesson_plans/music/

There are many lesson ideas and resources available at this Teach-nology site. The topics include composition, songs, vocal, drama/theater, and music lesson plans.

Kathy Schrock's Guide to the Arts

http://school.discovery.com/schrockguide/arts/artp.html

A high-quality selection of listings for dance, music, and drama are available at Kathy Schrock's site.

Photography

Exposure—A Beginners Guide to Photography

http://www.photonhead.com/beginners/

This site is great if you want your students to learn more about taking and working with photographs. Students can take a quick course in photography, learn a few tips on how to jazz up their photos, or use the Sim-Cam to learn how exposure and depth of field work.

Kodak: Taking Great Photos

http://www.kodak.com/eknec/PageQuerier.jhtml?pq-path=38andpq-locale=en_US

Kodak offers tips on taking pictures, using digital cameras, printing pictures, and sharing pictures online. The site provides photo projects on enhancing and restoring photos and creating inspirational photo stories. Your students will enjoy the way this site is set up and how easy it is for them to use.

Classroom Management

Introduction

Classroom management is an issue that all teachers face, no matter what grade level they teach. When giving any lesson, a teacher must have the attention and respect of his or her students in order for the lesson to be effective. Without proper management techniques, too much time that could be better spent teaching is spent disciplining and trying to gain control. Teachers have so many options when it comes to classroom management ideas, and creativity goes a long way. These are websites that provide useful and helpful ideas on anything from how to set up your classroom to proper discipline procedures. Also included in this list are character-building websites for teaching invaluable lessons that will transform your students sense of community within the classroom and their moral values and ethics.

SUGGESTED activity

Check out these sites yourself or with your colleagues and make a list of the techniques that might be useful to you. Write the ideas down on note cards and post them around your desk for quick reference. Do not try to make too many changes at one time. Select a couple that you think will make a big difference and attempt to integrate them into what you are doing. If they work, you might want to try more. Challenge your students to make management changes too.

Classroom Management (cont.)

General Ideas

NEA: In the Classroom—A Classroom Management Archive

http://www.nea.org/classmanagement/archive.html

The National Education Association site is a spectacular site. Their In the Classroom section has lesson ideas, classroom management suggestions, a Do the Right Thing link, teaching experience archive, a Works4Me, and a dropout prevention section. This site is great if you are a new classroom teacher. Reviewing the experiences of others should help you feel more comfortable. This site helps with the feeling all teachers have at one time or another: "I need to know more but I don't know whom or what to ask!"

A to Z Teacher Stuff

http://www.atozteacherstuff.com/index.shtml

This site has an excellent variety of resources for teachers. The following sections offer useful ideas for managing a classroom and working with students.

*A to Z Teacher Stuff—Classroom Management

http://www.atozteacherstuff.com/Tips/Classroom_Management/index.shtml

*A to Z Teacher Stuff—Classroom Jobs

http://www.atozteacherstuff.com/tips/Classroom_Jobs/

Education World Professional Development Center: Classroom Management

http://www.education-world.com/a_curr/archives/classmanagement.shtml

This site offers archived classroom management articles from its Professional Development Center. It offers a number of approaches from which to choose.

Education World Administrator's Center: Advice for First Year Teachers

http://www.educationworld.com/a_admin/admin/admin124.shtml

This link offers great advice from teachers who have survived their first year of teaching. Check it out for help with that first day in the classroom.

Classroom Management

Classroom Management [cont.]

General Ideas [cont.]

Teach Net—Power Tools—How to... Classroom Management

http://www.teachnet.com/how-to/manage/index.html

Teach Net's Power Tools section presents ideas and services that simplify teaching. From websites with tools to use online to simple tips that save you time, this site is worth checking out.

Kim's Korner for Teacher Talk—Classroom Management

http://www.kimskorner4teachertalk.com/classmanagement/menu.html

Kim's Korner Classroom Management section has ideas for many areas of classroom management. It currently includes tips for getting organized, bulletin boards, where to find inexpensive items, icebreakers, review games, simplifying the work load, activities for the first day, welcoming new teachers, rewards, and ideas for a postcard exchange.

Behavior Management

A to Z Teacher Stuff

http://www.atozteacherstuff.com/index.shtml

This is an excellent site with a variety of resources for teachers. The following sections specifically offer useful ideas for managing a classroom and working with students.

*A to Z Teacher Stuff—Managing Behavior

http://atozteacherstuff.com/Tips/Managing_Behavior/

*A to Z Teacher Stuff—Motivating Students

http://www.atozteacherstuff.com/Tips/Motivating_Students/index.shtml

NEA: Works4Me—Classroom Management—Behavior Control

http://www.nea.org/tips/manage/behavior.html

Works 4 Me, offered at the National Education Association's website, is a section from In the Classroom. It focuses specifically on classroom behavior issues by providing examples of teaching strategies that have worked for other teachers.

Classroom Management (cont.)

Dr. Mac's Amazing Behavior Management Advice Site

http://www.behavioradvisor.com/

This site has thousands of tips on managing student behavior. Plus, they have step-by-step directions for implementing many standard interventions. It also contains a bulletin board on which you can post disciplinary concerns and receive suggestions from teachers around the world. If you want lots of ideas and want to be able to compare and contrast several well-known and used strategies, then this is an excellent site to visit.

Ways to Catch Kids Being Good

http://maxweber.hunter.cuny.edu/pub/eres/EDSPC715_MCINTYRE/CatchGood.html

This website provides ideas to catch students while they are showing their best behavior in the classroom. It always helps to focus on positive classroom behaviors.

National Dissemination Center for Children with Disabilities—Behavior at School

http://www.nichcy.org/resources/behavschool.asp

This is a resource page from the National Dissemination Center for Children with Disabilities. They believe that "school presents a unique challenge for children with behavior issues. Teachers need tools to use to help provide support and guidance, and administrators need methods for creating a positive learning atmosphere within the entire school." NICHCY includes resources that will give teachers and schools the tools they need to create a safe and positive learning environment for all children. They also provide informed and positive behavior support for students who need special attention for their behavior problems.

National Network for Child Care—Managing Children's Behavior

http://www.nncc.org/Guidance/better.rules.html

This site offers basic information, but it is easy to follow and understand and is perfect for new teachers or for those that want to revisit ideas for managing a classroom.

Classroom Management [cont.]

Character Education

Character Education Partnership

http://www.character.org

Character Education Partnership is an organization for character education. It serves as the leading resource for people and organizations that are integrating character education into their schools and communities. CEP focuses on defining and encouraging effective practices and approaches to quality character education and provides a forum for the exchange of ideas. Based on research by the nation's leading character education experts, CEP's *Eleven Principles of Effective Character Education and Character Education Quality Standards* provide guidelines for the basics needed for a character education program.

Character Counts

http://www.charactercounts.org/

Character Counts is the most widely implemented approach to character education. Thousands of schools, communities, public agencies, and nonprofit groups are now using this program. It promotes the Six Pillars of Character—trustworthiness, respect, responsibility, fairness, caring, and citizenship. The national office develops and supports groups with training programs, special projects, materials, and consulting.

Good Character—Character Education

http://www.goodcharacter.com/

Every teacher can benefit from this site. Good Character offers programs and projects in several different areas of character education. The Good Character site provides teaching guides for grades K–12. The guides offer discussion questions, writing assignments, and student activities that you can use to create your own lesson plans. They also offer project-based learning activities to help develop good citizenship and community responsibility and provide tools to help coaches build good character in their sports program. Their opportunities for students to become involved in character-building activities are also very worthwhile.

Their selected Web pages contain practical material for character teachers. There is a lot in their pages that can be used as the basis for class discussions, writing assignments, and student activities. Their section related to work ethics is good to use with students who are getting ready to enter the workforce either on a part-time or full-time basis. They provide possible work-related scenarios that your students can discuss.

Classroom Management (cont.)

Character Education (cont.)

Positive Coaching Alliance

http://www.positivecoach.org/

Positive Coaching Alliance, a national nonprofit group based at Stanford University, is creating a movement to transform youth sports so that every youth athlete can have a positive character-building experience. PCA provides live and online workshops to train youth sports leaders, coaches, parents, and athletes on how to make sports a positive experience. At the core of their training are techniques that have been proven to improve athletic performance. They believe that "every child deserves a Double-Goal Coach, one who strives to win while achieving the second, more important goal of using sports to teach life lessons."

Center for the Advancement of Ethics and Character—Boston University

www.bu.edu/education/caec

This site includes excellent resources for teachers, parents, and administrators and provides a wide range of services and information and some very useful sample lessons.

The Giraffe Project

http://www.giraffe.org

The Giraffe Heroes Program honors people who "stick their necks out for the common good." This nonprofit organization tells "Giraffe Hero" stories. Giraffe Heroes are models for the rest of us. The Giraffe Heroes Program provides materials for schools and youth groups. There are great interactive resources for students. Encourage them to visit the For Kids Only section of the site. They can send a Giraffe-E Postcard from the Giraffe Heroes Project to any email address in their address book. The Giraffe-E Postcards have great quotes on courage, heroism, and compassion, and new quotes are added to their cards regularly.

Communicating Online: Blogs, Podcasts, Wikis, Discussion Boards, and Mailing Lists

Introduction

Blogs, podcasts, and wikis are new to many teachers. Think about what David Thornburg says, "If you bring in these (new) technologies and don't think ahead to how they'll be used to promote learning and the acquisition of skills, then the only thing that will change in school is the electric bill." Investigate new technologies. Do not use a new technology just because it is new. Use it because it will add to and broaden the experience of learning in your classroom. On the other hand, do not dismiss new technology either until you have given it a chance.

Blog is short for Web log. It is a web page that is an accessible interactive personal journal for the public to see and make comments on. There are blogs on a number of topics, and there are various formats that can be used in a blog, such as photographs (photoblog), video, and audio (podcasts). A wiki is a collaborative website that can be edited by anyone with access making the information provided in a wiki the work of multiple authors. Remember that due to the nature of these wikis, they may contain information that is inaccurate. A popular wiki site is Wikipedia at **http://en.wikipedia.org**. A discussion board allows you to share your ideas with others on a topic of interest.

SUGGESTED activity

Setting up a family blog would be a great activity for any student to nurture writing skills and learn more about the Internet. Ask each student to select something like a family vacation, a favorite holiday, a sport, or a homework project that he or she is doing at school for the topic of a blog. Help each student set up the blog on the website 21st Classes—Cooperative Learning **http://www.21classes.com/**. You can show him or her how to personalize the color and template and write a heading. Encourage each student to document the important events that happen and help with grammar and spelling so that it is an educational experience.

Communicating Online: Blogs, Podcasts, Wikis, Discussion Boards, and Mailing Lists [cont.]

Blogs

Google Blog

http://blogsearch.google.com/

Google has a specific search engine that will help you search for specific blogs related to topics of interest to you. This is a great place to explore what is out there in the new world of blogs.

Teacher Lingo

http://teacherlingo.com/

Teacher Lingo is a growing teacher community that connects teachers and educators from every level. It is a place where teachers can share ideas, ask questions, learn from one another, or even vent about their school day. At this site, you can create your free teacher blog, share your thoughts and ideas, personalize your blog, share photos, get connected to a family of teachers, and check out the message boards. Specific blog groups help you find posts and teachers at your grade level and with your interests.

Bud the Teacher—Inquiry and Reflection for Better Teaching

http://budtheteacher.typepad.com/

Bud Hunt teaches high school language arts and journalism at Olde Columbine High School in Longmont, Colorado. He is a teacher-consultant with the Colorado State University Writing Project, an affiliate of the National Writing Project. Its focus is to improve the teaching of writing in schools with professional development. Bud blogs and podcasts at **http://www.budtheteacher.com**. Check his blogs and podcasts to see what teachers are talking about in the area of teaching practices.

Bud the Teacher—Blogging Policies and Wiki Resources

http://budtheteacher.com/wiki/

Bud Hunt's students and fellow contributors have collected some of the best blogging resources at their wiki. Some are quite well developed, while others are still just the seeds of an idea that need some fleshing out. Since there is not much out there on blogging, this is a great place to start. If you have done some blogging, add your ideas to this wiki. This is a good site to check out what is happening in this new area of Internet technology.

Communicating Online

Communicating Online: Blogs, Podcasts, Wikis, Discussion Boards, and Mailing Lists *(cont.)*

Blogs *(cont.)*

Cool Cat Teacher Blog Spot

http://coolcatteacher.blogspot.com/

Cool Cat Teacher Blog Spot is a leading edublog that is written and managed by Vicki Davis. Vicki is a teacher, entrepreneur, edublogger, conference presenter, and freelance writer. She is a blogger for Tech Learning and a cofounder of Women of Web 2.0 and cohost of its weekly webcast at Ed Tech Talk. Check out her site to find out more about blogging and to get started in this interactive activity. This site was a 2006 EduBlog Award Winner.

Edtechtalk

http://www.edtechtalk.com/

EdTechTalk is a community of educators interested in discussing and learning about the uses of educational technology. The EdTechTalk Channel currently webcasts six shows: 21st Century Learning, EdTechBrainstorm, EdTechTalk, EdTechWeekly, Teachers Teaching Teachers, and Women of Web 2.0. During shows, listeners can use any common media player (i.e., *Windows Media Player, Real Player,* or *iTunes*) to listen to the discussion and use the chat room to make comments and ask questions. This is a great site for familiarizing yourself with podcasts and vblogs (video blogs).

A Difference Blog Spot

http://adifference.blogspot.com/

This is the blog site of a high school math teacher. It also won the 2006 EduBlog Award.

The Education Podcast Network

http://epnweb.org

Also connected to Landmarks for Schools, The Education Podcast Network is a directory of education-related podcast programs. This network is an effort to bring a range of podcast programming into one place. You can look for content to teach with and about and look at issues of teaching and learning in the 21st century. If you are interested in podcasting, visit this site.

Communicating Online

Communicating Online: Blogs, Podcasts, Wikis, Discussion Boards, and Mailing Lists [cont.]

Creating a Blog

21st Classes—Cooperative Learning

http://www.21classes.com/

Another site that offers teachers the opportunity to create a virtual classroom and a blog portal is 21st Classes—Cooperative Learning. Teachers can host and manage blogs for their students, use a class home page to communicate with students, and review the entries. Teachers can personalize their blogs by choosing from a variety of templates and customize them by uploading an individual header, changing colors and much more. Best of all, the site has advanced privacy settings and spam protection. This is a perfect site if you want to enter the world of blogging.

Landmarks for Schools

http://landmark-project.com/

Landmarks for Schools has more than six million page viewers a month from nearly one hundred countries. It includes tools for blogging and podcasting. It also offers resources for schools so they can set up their own blogs and podcasts.

Blogmeister

http://classblogmeister.com

Connected to Landmarks for Schools, the Blogmeister is especially suited for the classroom. This online blogging tool was explicitly designed with teachers and students in mind. You can evaluate, comment on, and finally publish students' blog articles in a controlled environment. Review "Establishing a Blogmeister Account PDF" at **http://classblogmeister.com/blogmeister_instructions.pdf** to learn about the requirements for setting up an account.

Ipodder.org

http://ipodder.org/

To subscribe to a podcast, you will need an aggregator. An aggregator is a website or software program that helps you organize podcast programs, blogs, and other syndicated (RSS) feeds. One program you can use is the iPodder program found at this site.

Communicating Online: Blogs, Podcasts, Wikis, Discussion Boards, and Mailing Lists [cont.]

Discussion Boards, Mailing Lists, and Web Rings

Teachers.Net Chatboard Network

http://teachers.net/mentors/

The Chatboard Network is a mentor support center that brings together hundreds of educators for peer support and development. Look at this site to see if you can take advantage of their incredible panel of experts. You will find wonderful resources and teacher support here.

Teacher's Guide to Listserves

http://www.theteachersguide.com/listservs.html

This site is hosted on the Teacher Created Resources site. It has instructions for joining a mailing list/listserve, and extensive links to different lists currently being hosted on the Internet.

The Teacher Net

http://teachers.net/mailrings/

This site has separate mailing lists for each grade, along with specialty rings. This site is considered one of the best resources for educational mailing lists.

Teachers.Net Webring

http://teachers.net/webring/

The Teachers.Net Webring is a network of teachers across the world, united through Teachers.Net! Teachers can show off their websites on the World Wide Web. Do you have a Web page of your own that you would like to show off? You can submit your website for inclusion on the Teachers.Net Webring and become a part of this collection of teacher resources.

Early Childhood Resources

Introduction

These sites offer resources specifically for the early childhood educator. The needs of young children are different from those of older children. Young children are just beginning to learn in a school environment with other children their own age. They require special instruction and attention to help them develop new skills intellectually, physically, and emotionally. They are working on motor skills, learning how to get along with others, learning letters and words, rhymes and nursery songs, and creating art, music, and dance, among other activities. These sites will provide you with a variety of resources, including lesson plans, interactive games, and learning situations that are standards based. There are also activity print outs and tips and advice for dealing with young children.

SUGGESTED activity

Check out The National Association for the Education of Young Children at **http://www.naeyc.org/** if you are not already an affiliate member. Look for ideas that will make your classroom activities more engaging, that will require your students to do more thinking, and will give them the ability to use all their senses as they work and play.

Early Childhood Resources [cont.]

Early Childhood References

National Association for the Education of Young Children

http://www.naeyc.org/

The National Association for the Education of Young Children (NAEYC) is a membership organization dedicated to "improving the well-being of all young children, with particular focus on the quality of educational and developmental services for all children from birth through age eight." NAEYC offers information on conferences, and specific resources for members, teachers, families, higher education, and students.

Quick Source

http://www.teacherquicksource.com/

Don't miss this site. You will find the process of finding curriculum-based activities that relate to standards, class goals, and objectives. They provide three areas for teachers to find quick resources.

Preschool Activity QuickSource is a convenient resource to help teachers find curriculum-based, developmentally appropriate activities and products correlated to NAEYC standards.

Head Start Activity QuickSource has activities that specifically support Head Start Child Outcomes and Head Start's Domain Curriculum Areas. Teachers can integrate the activities directly into their classroom activities.

Environmental Activity QuickSource provides resources to help you explore ways to educate children on the importance of caring for the environment and helping to make the earth a healthier place.

Education World—Early Childhood

http://www.education-world.com/a_earlychildhood/

This site has been created to support all those who are involved in the education of young children. Teachers, parents, aides, and administrators are encouraged to explore their resources and share their ideas for working with young children. This site keeps up with all that is new in education, so it is a good site to review regularly to keep up with what is happening in education. They also offer Education World's Early Childhood Education Newsletter. Each newsletter focuses on a theme of special interest to early childhood educators. Do not miss this site. There are sure to be many resources you can use.

Early Childhood

Early Childhood Resources (cont.)

Early Childhood References (cont.)

Gayles' Preschool Rainbow Activity Central

http://www.preschoolrainbow.org/

Gayles' Preschool Rainbow Activity Central offers preschool education activities and early childhood education lesson plans focused on giving preschool children choices as they learn. The ideas for classroom curriculum are arranged by theme. They also offer easy, at-home, fun learning games. Teachers can use a search function and can submit their own ideas. There is a small membership fee for using the whole site, but teachers can have free access by submitting five lesson plans. Get involved—give ideas and get many back!

PBS Teachers—Early Childhood

http://www.pbs.org/teachers/earlychildhood/

PBS provides early childhood educators with curriculum tools and professional resources. Their projects are curriculum standards-based and are both interesting and worthwhile.

A-Z Teacher Stuff—Lesson Plans

http://atozteacherstuff.com/Lesson_Plans/

A-Z Teacher Stuff has a new lesson plans directory. Teachers can search or browse lesson plans and teaching resources to find what they need for themes and thematic units, literature and book activities, math, science, learning centers, social studies, computers, reading, writing, P.E./health, cooperative learning, and more. What makes this site great for early childhood educators is that they can look by grade level, either preschool or K–2.

First School Preschool Activities and Crafts

http://www.first-school.ws/

First School features free, fun preschool lesson plans, educational early childhood activities, printable crafts, worksheets, a calendar of events, and other resources for children of preschool age. The preschool crafts, lesson plans, and activities are appropriate and adaptable for toddlers, preschoolers, and kindergarteners. This site is rich in resources.

Everything Preschool

http://www.everythingpreschool.com/

This site contains over 30,000 early childhood education ideas separated into over 100 themes, 26 alphabet idea sections and lesson plans, project recipes, bulletin board ideas, and a holiday calendar. Teachers will like the thoroughness of this site's topic coverage.

Early Childho

Early Childhood Resources (cont.)

Early Childhood References (cont.)

Family TLC

http://www.familytlc.net/

You can select a child's age group (babies through teens) to access family activities—games, sports, crafts, music, cooking, and nature. They offer parenting tips, articles on child development and hundreds of age-appropriate child activities each month. While this site is parent/child focused, it offers relevant resources to the early childhood teacher too. One of the best features of this site is that it also suggests several books that relate to the activities.

Literacy Center.Net—The Early Childhood Education Network

http://www.literacycenter.net/

This site offers hands-on computer literacy activities in four languages: English, Spanish, German, and French. The activities include upper- and lowercase letters, shapes, writing, words, numbers, colors, and keyboard. Check out the activities; they may be suitable for your students.

Education Laws and Standards

Introduction

These sites focus on the laws and standards that govern public education and programs for children. Schools and their teachers can be greatly affected by educational policy changes. The laws that have been passed in the United States in the past few years have impacted education across the nation. State Departments of Education also affect the focus of education in their states, which in turn affects what teachers must ultimately teach. Standards-based education offers a focus for creating curriculum, so it is important for teachers to keep up on what standards are expected to be met in their state. Teachers also need to know what testing policies and curriculum requirements are in place in their state. The sites here focus on these laws and standards, and they also deal with education-related legal issues and the rights that teachers, students, and their families have in the educational domain.

SUGGESTED activity

Review and study up on the No Child Left Behind Act at this government site: **http://www.ed.gov/nclb/landing.jhtml?src=pb**. This site provides the details of this act and how this new law affects teachers and schools. Share your knowledge with other teachers who may not know what this act is all about and what the issues are. Offer to lead a discussion of the act's topics at one of your school's staff meetings. Include the benefits of the act as well as possible concerns that you and your colleagues might have. An open forum can provide a way to express opinions and ideas that can improve curriculum and help with test preparation for those looming assessments that your students need to take.

Education Laws and Standards [cont.]

Educational Standards

Education World—National Education Standards

http://www.education-world.com/standards/national/

Several national education organizations have taken on the challenge of creating educational standards or guidelines to be used on a national level. They include the following:

National Council of Teachers of Mathematics

http://www.nctm.org/

National Council of Teachers of English

http://www.ncte.org/

National Council for Social Studies

http://www.ncss.org/

National Center for History in the Schools

http://www.sscnet.ucla.edu/nchs/

International Society for Technology in Education

http://cnets.iste.org/index.html

National Academies of Science

http://www.nas.edu/

Education World—State Education Standards

http://www.education-world.com/standards/state/index.shtml

Find quick access to all the state standards by using a pull-down menu at this site and choosing a state.

Education Laws and Standards (cont.)

Laws Affecting Students

ED.gov

http://www.ed.gov/index.jhtml

ED.gov was created in 1980 by combining offices from several federal agencies. Its original directive remains its mission today—"to ensure equal access to education and to promote educational excellence throughout the nation." ED.gov is dedicated to:

- Establishing policies on federal financial aid for education and distributing as well as monitoring those funds

- Collecting data on America's schools and disseminating research

- Focusing national attention on key educational issues

- Prohibiting discrimination and ensuring equal access to education

This site offers excellent resources for administrators, teachers, parents, and students.

No Child Left Behind

http://www.ed.gov/nclb/landing.jhtml?src=pb

President George W. Bush signed the No Child Left Behind Act on January 8, 2002. This law was designed to help schools improve by focusing on accountability for results, freedom for states and communities, proven education methods, and choices for parents. This site provides a link to an A–Z Index to help you find your way around the NCLB section. It includes policy proposals and documents on accountability, choice, teacher quality, and other elementary/secondary policy issues. It also includes links to "What the President's budget means for your state" and "How NCLB is making a difference in your state." Find your state contacts and check out the tools and resources that are provided for making informed decisions to improve student performance.

Individuals with Disabilities Education

http://idea.ed.gov/

The Individuals with Disabilities Education Act (IDEA) is a law that ensures services to children with disabilities throughout the nation. IDEA governs how states and public agencies provide early intervention, special education, and related services to more than 6.5 million eligible infants, toddlers, children, and youth with disabilities. Children and youth (ages 3–21) receive special education and related services under IDEA Part B. Infants and toddlers with disabilities (birth–2) and their families receive early intervention services under IDEA Part C. This site provides details about this law and its resources for educators and parents.

Education Laws and Standards (cont.)

Laws Affecting Teachers

Family Educational Rights and Privacy Act (FERPA)

http://www.ed.gov/policy/gen/guid/fpco/index.html

The Family Educational Rights and Privacy Act (FERPA) is a federal law that protects the privacy of student education records. The law applies to all schools that receive funds under an applicable program of the U.S. Department of Education.

Fair Labor Standards

http://www.dol.gov/esa/whd/flsa/

The Fair Labor Standards Act (FLSA) establishes minimum wage, overtime pay, record keeping, and child labor standards affecting full-time and part-time workers in the private sector and in federal, state, and local governments. This site provides information about this law and how it relates to working individuals.

Family and Medical Leave

http://www.dol.gov/esa/whd/fmla/

Covered employers (public as well as private elementary and secondary schools are covered employers) must grant an eligible employee up to a total of 12 workweeks of unpaid leave during any 12-month period. The reason for leave must be the birth and care of a newborn child of the employee; the placement with the employee of a son or daughter for adoption or foster care; the care for an immediate family member with a serious health condition; or the need to take medical leave when the employee is unable to work because of a serious health condition. This site provides information about how this law relates to educators.

Foundations and Grant-Providing Organizations

Introduction

Education environments are always in need of additional funding. Whether schools are attempting to provide basic supplies for their students, give teachers further training, or provide special programs to enhance learning, there is never enough funding for it all. This guide provides a wide range of resources that teachers and administrators can use to research what support is out there for them.

A brief description of the goals or focus provided by each agency is included. Hopefully this is sufficient to let you decide if the organization has anything that can help your particular teaching environment.

SUGGESTED activity

Check out the following Teacher Created Materials book: *The Educator's Guide to Grants for Special Education, Intervention and Specialized Programs, and Professional Development* at **http://www.teachercreatedmaterials.com/estore/product/3435**.

This book is designed for educators who know the basics of grant writing and are ready to go after larger, more specific grants for intervention and remedial programs, special education, physical education, technology, the arts, and professional development. Dr. Linda Karges-Bone is an educator, author, and consultant who wrote and was awarded her first grant when she was still a teenager. She specializes in grant writing for schools and nonprofit groups. In this book she shares techniques for designing a grant in a specific area of need, a step-by-step timeline for on-time submission, tips for applying online for e-grants, and a carefully screened list of funding sources.

Foundations and Grant-Providing Organizations [cont.]

Foundations and Grants

Grants Alert

http://www.grantsalert.com/

The number one goal at GrantsAlert.com is to make life a little easier for those who are searching for educational grants and trying to identify new funding opportunities for their organization, school, district, or state education agencies. Site visitors can browse through their list of grants currently available, participate in Grant Alerts Blog, or get help with writing grants from the Grant Writers' Directory.

Education World Grant Writing Tips—Show Me the Money: Tips and Resources for Successful Grant Writing

http://www.educationworld.com/a_curr/profdev/profdev039.shtml

Many educators have found that outside funding, in the form of grants, allows them to provide their students with educational experiences and materials their own districts cannot afford. At Education World, you can learn how they get those grants and how you might be able to get one too.

Education World Administrators Grant Center

http://www.education-world.com/a_admin/archives/grants.shtml

This is another section on the Education World site related to grants. It is directed to administrators but has valuable information for any educator. It has Current Grants, More Grant Sources, and Grant Help sections.

Eduscapes—Grant and Grant Writing

http://www.eduscapes.com/tap/topic94.htm

This site is a good site to give you ideas about what is available and how you might use the resources out there to your class's or school's advantage. Its major topics include Grant Resources Starting Points, Exploring Grant Possibilities, Getting Started, Identifying the Need and Your Solution: Goal Setting, Writing a Grant Proposal, Submitting Your Grant, Assessing the Process, and Identifying Funding Sources.

#50475—Must-See Websites for Busy Teachers

Foundations and Grant-Providing Organizations *(cont.)*

Foundations and Grants *(cont.)*

Teachers Network—Teacher Grants

http://teachersnetwork.org/grants/

Teachers Network has compiled a series of grant opportunities for various topics. They have organized the site by areas of interest, school curriculum areas, and help topics.

Top Teaching Resources—Grant and Funding Resources

http://www.topteachingresources.com/grants_funding.php

Merit Software sponsors this site. It lists and describes many of the grant and funding resources available to schools.

SchoolGrants.org

http://www.schoolgrants.org/

SchoolGrants was created in 1999 as a way to share grant information and grant writing tips with Pre-K–12 educators. The site states that "Grant writing can be intimidating to those who are new at it." Finding suitable grant opportunities requires a great deal of time and research. SchoolGrants.org reduces this effort by listing a variety of opportunities that are available to public and private nonprofit elementary and secondary schools and districts across the United States.

Foundation Center

http://foundationcenter.org/

Established in 1956 and supported today by more than 600 foundations, the Foundation Center is the nation's leading authority on philanthropy, connecting nonprofits and grant makers and supporting them with tools and information they can use. The center maintains the most comprehensive database on U.S. grant makers and their grants. They also operate research, education, and training programs designed to advance philanthropy at every level. More than 37,000 people visit this website each day, and thousands more are served in their five regional library/learning centers.

Foundations and Grant- Providing Organizations [cont.]

Foundations and Grants [cont.]

Bill and Melinda Gates Foundation—Education

http://www.gatesfoundation.org/UnitedStates/Education/

Through its partnerships in communities across the United States, the Bill and Melinda Gates Foundation is committed to raising the high school graduation rate and helping all students—regardless of race or family income—graduate ready for college and work. They also work to provide children with opportunities for quality early learning.

David and Lucille Packard Foundation

http://www.packard.org/home.aspx

Guided by the business philosophy and values of their founders, the David and Lucille Packard Foundation helps people and organizations improve the lives of children, pursue science, investigate reproductive health, and conserve and restore earth's natural resources. The foundation has a grant-making budget of approximately $248 million for 2007. Their Children, Families, and Communities Program looks for opportunities for children to reach their potentials.

Tiger Woods Foundation

http://www.twfound.org/

The Tiger Woods Foundation helps children reach their dreams through enrichment programs, scholarships, direct grants, junior golf teams and the new Tiger Woods Learning Center. The Tiger Woods Foundation grants focus on providing opportunities to underserved youth ages 5–17. Their average grant range is between $2,500 and $25,000. They focus on programs that enhance the learning process for youth, offer mentoring and tutoring programs, and are based in urban American cities.

Marco Polo Education Foundation

http://www.marcopolo-education.org/

The Marco Polo Education Foundation provides standards-based content in a variety of disciplines. The content includes lesson plans and training materials to help teachers integrate Internet content into their classwork.

Foundations and Grant-Providing Organizations [cont.]

Foundations and Grants [cont.]

National Academy Foundation (NAF)

http://www.naf.org

National Academy Foundation is a nationwide network of career-themed academies for high school students. NAF students remain together throughout their high school years with a core group of specially trained teachers. There are more than 529 career academies nationwide that include academies of finance, hospitality and tourism, and information technology. You might see this approach to school as the perfect opportunity for some of your students, or you may want to look at their "small community" as a possible model that may enhance the programs you are offering students at your school.

National Center on Education and the Economy

http://www.ncee.org

The National Center on Education and the Economy is dedicated to providing the policies, tools, and technical assistance that schools, districts, and states need to become leaders in education and training.

National Education Association Foundation for the Improvement of Education

http://www.neafoundation.org/

http://www.neafoundation.org/grants.htm

The NEA Foundation for the Improvement of Education "inspires public education employees to ensure that all students succeed." Through a variety of grants, the NEA Foundation supports efforts by teachers, education support professionals, and higher-education faculty and staff to improve student learning in the nation's public schools, colleges, and universities.

Foundations and Grants

Foundations and Grant-Providing Organizations [cont.]

Foundations and Grants [cont.]

National Endowment for the Arts

http://www.nea.gov/

http://www.nea.gov/Grants/index.html

The National Endowment for the Arts is a public agency dedicated to supporting excellence in the arts. They work on bringing the arts to the general public, and they provide leadership in arts education. Congress established the National Endowment for the Arts in 1965 as an independent agency of the federal government. The Endowment is the nation's largest annual provider to the arts. It brings great art to all 50 states, including rural areas, inner cities, and military bases.

National Endowment for the Humanities

http://www.neh.gov/

http://www.neh.gov/grants/index.html

National Endowment for the Humanities is like the National Endowment for the Arts. It is an independent grant-making agency of the United States government that is dedicated to supporting research, education, preservation, and public programs in the humanities.

Annenberg Foundation

http://www.whannenberg.org/

The Annenberg Foundation's focus is on the restructuring and reform of grades K through 12. Its major program areas are education and youth development; arts and culture; civic organizations; community and the environment; and health and human services. The Foundation encourages the development of more effective ways to share ideas and knowledge.

National Foundation for the Improvement of Education

http://www.nfie.org/

The National Foundation for the Improvement of Education provides grants and assistance to teachers, education support personnel, and higher-education faculty and staff to improve student learning in the nation's public schools.

Foundations and Grant-Providing Organizations [cont.]

Foundations and Grants [cont.]

Christensen Fund

http://www.christensenfund.org

The Christensen Fund is a private institution dedicated to assisting organizations in the arts, natural sciences, and education.

Self-Education Foundation

http://www.selfeducation.org/

Self-Education Foundation supports individual and community self-education through grant making, community organizing, and outreach.

Foundation Infantia

http://www.infantia.org/

Foundation Infantia works to restore, construct, and improve school centers in developing nations.

Gladys Brooks Foundation

http://www.gladysbrooksfoundation.org/

The Gladys Brooks Foundation promotes intellectual, moral, and physical welfare by establishing and supporting nonprofit libraries, educational institutions, hospitals, and clinics.

Jimmy and Rosalynn Carter Partnership Foundation

http://www.jrcpf.org/

The Jimmy and Rosalynn Carter Partnership Foundation is an organization dedicated to fostering campus-community partnerships for academic service and learning.

Foundations and Grant-Providing Organizations [cont.]

Foundations and Grants [cont.]

Laura Bush Foundation for America's Libraries

http://www.laurabushfoundation.org/

The Laura Bush Foundation for America's Libraries provides grants to purchase books for school libraries across the country. It is a component of the Community Foundation for the National Capital Region in Washington.

Comprehensive Regional Assistance Centers

http://www.ed.gov/programs/newccp/index.html

This program awards discretionary grants to establish technical assistance centers that help low-performing schools and districts close achievement gaps and meet the goals of the No Child Left Behind Act of 2001.

First Book

http://www.firstbook.org/

First Book is a nonprofit organization with a single mission: to give children from low-income families the opportunity to read and own their first new books. Visit their website to get involved with starting a local chapter or to find out how to get books for children in need.

TrueGift Donations

http://www.truegift.com/

TrueGift Donations is a Nonprofit 501 corporation implementing direct contributions of school supplies to individual teachers.

Technology Funding

http://www.mcrel.org/lesson-plans/funding.asp

McRel.org has collected a set of links that will provide teachers with resources and ideas to find funding to support their technology education program. This site is well worth the visit.

Government Resources

Introduction

Government websites offer valuable information about the government, its agencies, programs available to educators, and excellent classroom resources. Sites have been included for the United States, Canada, and Mexico. The listing of the state and provincial departments of education provide links to the local governments that control public education. Standards, excellent lesson plans, and online activities are all available for teacher and classroom use.

SUGGESTED activity

Find the Department of Education for your state or province. Visit the site and familiarize yourself with the content available to you. Share this information with others in your teaching environment. Look for resources that you can use in your classroom. Select a site from this section that you feel will relate to your curriculum and that you can share with your students and their parents. Create a homework enrichment activity that will use the site and encourage parent-child interaction. Encourage them to explore and learn together. A good site to visit is the National Science Foundation where you can see their classroom resources page at **http://nsf.gov/news/classroom**. Here you will find great links to sites with lesson plans and learning opportunities for your students.

Government

Government Resources (cont.)

General Reference

U.S.A. Government Web Portal

http://www.usa.gov/

This site provides a variety of ways to get general and service information about the United States government. It includes sections for specific audiences. The ones most pertinent to teachers are the sections for Teachers and Educators, Kids and Youth, Parents, Librarians and Researchers, and Persons with Disabilities.

Free Federal Resources for Educational Excellence

http://www.free.ed.gov/index.cfm

The Teacher and Educators section provides free federal resources for educational excellence materials in the areas of science, math, social studies, and language arts. This is an excellent classroom resource and should not be missed. The math section offers activities for the classroom and for home use. It offers opportunities for families to become involved in learning math concepts.

Kids and Youth

http://www.kids.gov/

This site is the U.S. government interagency Kids' Portal. It was developed and is maintained by the Federal Citizen Information Center. It provides links to federal kids' sites along with some of the best kids' sites from other organizations. These sites are grouped by subject. Kids can explore, learn, and have fun at this safe site.

Ben's Guide to U.S. Government Website for Kids

✶ *http://bensguide.gpo.gov/subject.html*

This site provides links to government sites for kids that are divided by grade levels: K–2, 3–5, 6–8, 9–12, and sites for teachers and parents. Topic sections include Our Nation, Our Government, Your Neighborhood, Ben's ABCs, Symbols of U.S. Government, Games and Activities, and U.S. Government Websites for Kids. This site is well worth a visit.

Welcome to the White House

http://www.whitehouse.gov/

This site offers up-to-date information about what is happening in the White House. It includes the latest news and issues and offers the visitor the ability to interact through email with members of the White House staff.

Government Resources [cont.]

General Reference [cont.]

White House History and Tours

http://www.whitehouse.gov/history/life/video/index.html

This section of the White House site focuses on White House history and tours of the White House. The virtual tours, directed by the president and first lady, are the next best thing to being at the White House.

The White House for Kids

http://www.whitehouse.gov/kids/

This interactive presentation of information, specifically designed for kids, is a perfect place for students to learn about the White House and the history of the presidents of the United States. It is a fun place for kids to explore.

U.S. Senate

http://www.senate.gov

This site offers up-to-date information about the U.S. Senate, senators, committees, legislation, and records. There is also a history and art section and information for those planning a visit to the Capitol buildings.

U.S. House of Representatives

http://www.house.gov

This site offers up-to-date information about the U.S. House of Representatives, individual representatives, committees, legislation, and records. There is a section specifically designed to inform kids about the process of government.

U.S. Executive Branch Web Sites

http://www.loc.gov/rr/news/fedgov.html

This site contains executive branch sites only. Agencies are often included because they requested to be listed. For more government sites see:

- legislative branch sites at **http://thomas.loc.gov/home/legbranch/legbranch.html**
- judicial legislative branch sites at **http://www.uscourts.gov/**
- government resources in general at **http://www.loc.gov/rr/news/extgovd.html**

Government

General Reference [cont.]

State and Local Government on the Net

http://www.statelocalgov.net/

The State and Local Government Internet directory provides convenient one-stop access to the websites of thousands of state agencies and city and county governments. This is a good site for students to use when they do state reports or are studying the states and comparing their similarities and differences.

ED—U.S. Department of Education—Promoting Educational Excellence for all Americans

http://www.ed.gov/

ED was created in 1980 to ensure equal access to education and to promote educational excellence throughout the nation. The ED is dedicated to establishing policies on federal financial aid for education and distributing as well as monitoring those funds, collecting data on America's schools and disseminating research, focusing national attention on key educational issues, prohibiting discrimination, and ensuring equal access to education.

Comprehensive Regional Assistance Center

http://www.ed.gov/programs/newccp/index.html

This program awards discretionary grants to establish comprehensive technical assistance centers that help low-performing schools and districts close achievement gaps and meet the goals of the No Child Left Behind Act of 2001.

Education Resource Organizations Directory

http://www.ed.gov/erod/

The Education Resource Organizations Directory (EROD) contains information on more than 3,000 national, regional, and state education organizations, including many associations that provide information and assistance on a broad range of education-related topics.

Government Resources [cont.]

General Reference [cont.]

Federal Agency Directory

http://www.lib.lsu.edu/gov/fedgov.html

This directory is a partnership of Louisiana State University and the Federal Depository Library Program. It is an extensive list of all government departments, agencies, and programs.

Library of Congress

http://www.loc.gov/index.html

The Library of Congress is the nation's oldest federal institution. It is the research arm of Congress. It contains resource sections for teachers, librarians, and kids and parents. All teachers and students should become familiar with this site.

National Archives

http://www.archives.gov/

This government site has a teacher-student section featuring a digital classroom—the National Archives' gateway for resources about primary sources, activities, and training for educators and students. Don't miss this site!

National Science Foundation

http://www.nsf.gov/

The National Science Foundation is an independent U.S. government agency responsible for promoting science and engineering through research programs and education projects.

The Classroom Resources section, **http://www.nsf.gov/news/classroom/,** offers a diverse collection of lessons and Web resources for classroom teachers, their students, and their families. Materials are arranged by subject area to help you find resources of interest more easily.

Government

Government Resources [cont.]

American State Departments of Education

Alabama Department of Education

http://www.alsde.edu/html/home.asp

Alaska Department of Education and Early Development

http://www.eed.state.ak.us/

Arizona Department of Education

http://www.ade.az.gov/

Arkansas Department of Education

http://ArkansasEd.org

California Department of Education

http://www.cde.ca.gov/

Colorado Department of Education

http://www.cde.state.co.us/

Connecticut Department of Education

http://www.state.ct.us/sde/

Delaware Department of Education

http://www.doe.state.de.us/

District of Columbia Public Schools

http://www.k12.dc.us/dcps/home.html

Florida Department of Education

http://www.fldoe.org/

Government Resources [cont.]

American State Departments of Education [cont.]

Georgia Department of Education

http://public.doe.k12.ga.us/

Hawaii Department of Education

http://doe.k12.hi.us/

Idaho Department of Education

http://www.sde.state.id.us/Dept/

Illinois State Board of Education

http://www.isbe.net/

Indiana Department of Education

http://www.doe.state.in.us/

Iowa Department of Education

http://www.state.ia.us/educate/

Kansas Department of Education

http://www.ksde.org/

Kentucky Department of Education

http://www.education.ky.gov

Louisiana Department of Education

http://www.louisianaschools.net/lde/index.html

Maine Department of Education

http://www.maine.gov/portal/education/

Government

Government Resources [cont.]

American State Departments of Education [cont.]

Maryland Department of Education

http://www.marylandpublicschools.org/MSDE

Massachusetts Department of Education

http://www.doe.mass.edu/

Michigan Department of Education

http://www.michigan.gov/mde/

Minnesota Department of Education

http://education.state.mn.us/mde/index.html

Mississippi Department of Education

http://www.mde.k12.ms.us/

Missouri Department of Elementary and Secondary Education

http://dese.mo.gov/

Montana Office of Public Instruction

http://www.opi.mt.gov/

Nebraska Department of Education

http://www.nde.state.ne.us/

Nevada Department of Education

http://www.doe.nv.gov/

New Hampshire Department of Education

http://www.ed.state.nh.us

American State Departments of Education [cont.]

New Jersey Department of Education

http://www.state.nj.us/education/

New Mexico Public Education Department

http://www.ped.state.nm.us/

New York State Education Department

http://www.nysed.gov/

North Carolina Department of Public Instruction

http://www.ncpublicschools.org/

North Dakota Department of Public Instruction

http://www.dpi.state.nd.us/

Ohio Department of Education

http://www.ode.state.oh.us/

Oklahoma State Department of Education

http://sde.state.ok.us/

Oregon Department of Education

http://www.ode.state.or.us/

Pennsylvania Department of Education

http://www.pde.state.pa.us/

Rhode Island Department of Elementary and Secondary Education

http://www.ridoe.net/

Government

Government Resources

American State Departments of Education [cont.]

South Carolina Department of Education

http://www.myscschools.com/

South Dakota Department of Education

http://doe.sd.gov/

Tennessee State Department of Education

http://www.state.tn.us/education/

Texas Education Agency

http://www.tea.state.tx.us/

Utah State Office of Education

http://www.schools.utah.gov/

Vermont Department of Education

http://www.education.vermont.gov

Virginia Department of Education

http://www.doe.virginia.gov/

Washington Office of Superintendent of Public Instruction

http://www.k12.wa.us/

West Virginia Department of Education

http://wvde.state.wv.us/

Wisconsin Department of Public Instruction

http://www.dpi.state.wi.us/

Government Resources [cont.]

American State Departments of Education [cont.]

Wyoming Department of Education

http://www.k12.wy.us/

Guam Public School System

http://www.gdoe.net/

Puerto Rico Department of Education

http://www.gobierno.pr/GPRPortal/Inicio/EducacionEInvestigacion/DE.html

Virgin Islands

http://www.doe.vi/

Canada

The Government of Canada Page

http://canada.gc.ca/

This official government site for Canada has news and updates regarding the prime minister, governor general, Parliament, and Supreme Court. You can visit pages on any of Canada's departments and agencies, and there are links to websites affiliated with them as well. There are rich resources concerning many aspects of Canadian life in the About Canada section. If you are a tourist, you can go to the tourism link to get travel resources among other useful things.

Unofficial Web Site of Canada—The Canadian Resource Page

http://www.cs.cmu.edu/Unofficial/Canadiana/

A great many resources are listed on this site. Some of the sections include News and Information, Facts and Figures, Travel and Tourism, Government Services, Politics and History, Science and Education, Technology, Commerce and Industry and Heritage, and Culture and Industry. This is a great site for students who need to do a report on Canada.

Government

Government Resources [cont.]

Canadian Departments of Education

Alberta: Alberta Education

http://ednet.edc.gov.ab.ca/

Alberta Advanced Education and Career Development

http://www.learning.gov.ab.ca/

British Columbia: Ministry of Education

http://www.gov.bc.ca/bvprd/bc/channel.do?action=ministryandchannelID=-8382andnavId=NAV_ID_-8382

Manitoba: Manitoba Education and Training

http://www.edu.gov.mb.ca/

New Brunswick: Department of Education

http://www.gnb.ca/0000/index-e.asp

Newfoundland and Labrador: Department of Education

http://www.gov.nf.ca/edu/

Nova Scotia: Department of Education and Culture

http://www.ednet.ns.ca/

Nunavut: Government of Nunavut

http://www.gov.nu.ca/

Northwest Territories: Department of Education, Culture, and Employment

http://www.gov.nt.ca/agendas/education/index.html

Ontario: Ministry of Education

http://www.edu.gov.on.ca/eng/welcome.html

Canadian Departments of Education (cont.)

Québec: Ministère de l'Éducation

http://www.meq.gouv.qc.ca/

Saskatchewan: Saskatchewan Education

http://www.sasked.gov.sk.ca/

Yukon: Yukon Education

http://www.education.gov.yk.ca/

Ministry of Advanced Education

http://www.gov.bc.ca/bvprd/bc/channel.do?action=ministryandchannelID=-8376andnavId=NAV_ID_-8376

Department of Training and Employment Development

http://www.gnb.ca/0105/index-e.asp

Mexico

Official Mexican Government Information Site

http://www.gob.mx/wb/egobierno/egob_General_Information

This is a great resource for information about Mexico. Some of its topics include Government of the States, International Politics, Maps of the Mexican Republic, the Mexican Presidency, and Mexico the Country. There is also a great section on tourism that highlights why Mexico has become such a popular tourist destination.

President of Mexico—Official Site

http://www.presidencia.gob.mx/en/

This site reports on the activities of the president. From a political point of view, it is interesting to learn about current political issues and the influence the president has on Mexico's politics. This site also links to other important government resources.

Health and Physical Education Resources

Introduction

This section focuses on physical education and health programs. The recent national focus on the increase in childhood obesity has made teachers more aware of teaching students about healthy eating and exercising. Health education has always been a part of education but not all classroom teachers realized the necessity for it. These sites will offer resources for physical education teachers as well as general classroom teachers.

SUGGESTED activity

The Center for Nutrition Policy and Promotion, an organization of the U.S. Department of Agriculture, was established in 1994 to improve the nutrition and well-being of Americans. The center's core products to support its objectives are the following: Dietary Guidelines for Americans, My Pyramid Food Guidance System, Healthy Eating Index, U.S. Food Plans, Nutrient Content of the U.S. Food Supply, and Expenditures on Children by Families. All students can benefit from learning more about the Food Pyramid and their nutritional and physical activity needs. Visit this site: My Pyramid at **http://www.mypyramid.gov/** and go to the For Kids section. Select and print the My Pyramid for Kids poster. Choose the poster that is age appropriate for your students, either younger students or advanced elementary students. Discuss the food pyramid and its meaning with your students. If you want your students to discover more, allow them to go to Inside the Pyramid, use the My Pyramid Plan and look at the Tips and Resources. You can also print out the My Pyramid for Kids worksheet and have them track the foods they eat in one day. You can then discuss their choices and help them learn how to make good, healthy choices.

© Shell Education

Health

Health and Physical Education
Resources [cont.]

Health Program Resources

Kathy Schrock—Health and Fitness Resources

http://school.discovery.com/schrockguide/health/fitness.html

Kathy Schrock has assembled good resources, especially in the areas of health and nutrition.

Lesson Plans Page—P.E. and Health

http://www.lessonplanspage.com/PE.htm

Teachers can choose health and physical education lessons by grade level, recent additions, or seasonal lesson plans by date.

Teachers.Net—Health Lesson Plans

http://www.teachers.net/cgi-bin/lessons/sort.cgi?searchterm=Health

This health site is part of teachers.net lesson exchange. Teachers.Net offers lesson plans sorted by subject level, and it allows users to search for a lesson, submit a lesson, or request a lesson.

Discovery School—Health Lesson Plans

http://school.discovery.com/lessonplans/health.html

Lesson plans for health are divided into kindergarten–fifth grade, sixth–eigth grade, and ninth–twelfth grade level groupings. Many health and development topics are included in their list.

Lesson Plan Central—Health

http://lessonplancentral.com/lessons/Health/

This site provides lesson plans, WebQuests, worksheets, student links, and clipart for the topic of health education. You should also check out the health-related worksheet section of the site. It is located at **http://lessonplancentral.com/lessons/Health/Printables_and_Activities/index.htm**.

Health

Health and Physical Education
Resources [cont.]

(Healthy Eating)

My Pyramid

http://www.mypyramid.gov/

Using the program provided here, students can figure out the amount from each food group they need each day. A student can enter his or her own personal information and receive a customized food guide. Students can view their results online, or they can view and print a PDF version of their results. They can also view and print a helpful meal tracking worksheet. Then, if they want a more detailed assessment of their diet quality and physical activity, they can go to the My Pyramid Tracker. This site has resources for teachers, parents, and students. The For Kids section includes an interactive game, posters, worksheets, and other fun activities geared to help 6–11-year-olds understand their nutritional needs. This is a great site for all students.

USDA—US Agriculture Research Service—Children's Nutrition Research Center

http://www.kidsnutrition.org/consumer/archives/

The Children's Nutrition Research Center (CNRC) is dedicated to "defining the nutrient needs of children, from conception through adolescence, and the needs of pregnant women and nursing mothers." The scientific data from the center will help health care providers and policy advisors make dietary recommendations. This site provides an archive of materials grouped into nearly 60 categories. Some of the topics include Anemia, Body Weight, Body Fat, Breakfast, Childhood Obesity, Daycare Nutrition, Diabetes, Dieting, and Eating Habits, Energy Requirements, Food Composition, Food Guide Pyramid, Food Label, Food Safety, Milk/Milk Substitutes, Physical Activity, Picky Eaters, School Lunches, Snacking, Sports Drinks, and Sugar. This site is a great place to research any nutrition-related topic that you might come across with your students. It is an excellent site for nutrition reports and should not be missed.

Kidsnutrition.org—Healthy Eating

http://www.kidsnutrition.org/consumer/nyc/healthyeating.htm

This site is part of the USDA/ARS Children's Nutrition Research Center at Baylor College of Medicine. It has a Healthy Eating section that offers resources for the following topics: general nutrition information, help on feeding children, teaching nutrition, helping overweight children, eating disorders, physical activity and sports nutrition, vegetarianism, calcium nutrition/osteoporosis, and folic acid.

Health

Health and Physical Education Resources [cont.]

Healthy Eating [cont.]

FoodFit.com

http://www.foodfit.com/

FoodFit is part of Health Central. They have interactive tools to assess your current health habits, and a database of 2,500 healthy, customizable recipes with in-depth nutritional analysis. They also have hundreds of suggestions for celebrating foods of the seasons with their Season's Pick and their guide to seasonal foods. Their fitness section can help you get motivated, keep up on fitness trends, and get information to help you create your own workouts. To use their interactive tools, you will need to join, but memberships are now free.

Dole 5-A-Day

http://www.dole5aday.com/

Dole 5-a-Day currently has sections for kids, teachers, family and friends, the food service industry, and the media. It has been an excellent site for more than 12 years. The site is changing. It will keep its best information, add more current material, expand their site to include parents and bilingual visitors, provide resources to address the obesity crisis, and add new features to the site, like a newsletter. Besides all the wonderful resources for teachers, kids love to visit this site, sing their songs, use their resources, and participate in their activities.

Fruits and Veggies—More Matters

http://www.fruitsandveggiesmorematters.org/

This site offer great resources too. They want to get everyone eating more healthy foods. Its Get Kids Involved and Healthy Resources sections are worthwhile.

Health Central Network

http://www.healthcentral.com/

The Health Central Network, Inc. has a collection of websites and multimedia partners that provide in-depth and trusted medical information. They offer personalized tools and resources and connections to a community of experts for patients and people wanting to understand, manage and improve their health. This site contains valuable medical information and ideas for healthy living.

Health

Health and Physical Education
Resources [cont.]

Physical Education Program Resources

The American Alliance for Health, Physical Education, Recreation, and Dance (AAHPERD)

http://www.aahperd.org/index.cfm

The American Alliance for Health, Physical Education, Recreation, and Dance (AAHPERD) is the largest organization of professionals supporting those involved in physical education, leisure, fitness, dance, health promotion, education, and all specialties related to achieving a healthy lifestyle. AAHPERD supports healthy lifestyles through high-quality programs. This is an important organization for those who are involved in any of their professional groups.

National Standards for Physical Education

http://www.aahperd.org/naspe/publications-nationalstandards.html

Use this site to give you a listing of the national standards for physical education. It would be very easy to print and keep as a ready reference for planning your physical education program.

PE 4 Life

http://www.pe4life.org/

P.E.4LIFE is a national nonprofit advocacy organization for promoting quality daily physical education programs for America's youth. A free community action kit is available for the price of postage. The P.E.4LIFE: Community Action Kit includes *PowerPoint* presentations, handouts, sample letters, and a dynamic seven-minute video that highlights the benefits of quality physical education.

PE Central

http://www.pecentral.org/index.html

PE Central is a great website for health and physical education teachers, parents, and students. Their goal is to provide the latest information about developmentally appropriate physical education programs for children and youth. To combat the high obesity rate, they offer programs like Log It, The Coleman Everest 5.5 Challenge, and Get Active—Stay Active where students can log their physical activity and use a pedometer to track their steps. Their resources include assessments, health and physical education lesson ideas, job announcements, links to the top sport and instructional sites on the web, wellness tips, and instant activities that change on a weekly basis.

Health and Physical Education Resources [cont.]

Physical Education Program Resources [cont.]

Sports Media—P.E. Links Database

http://www.sports-media.org/links/data/index.html

This site offers lesson plans and coaching for more than 44 sports. It also offers resources for adaptive P.E, stretching, warming up, CPR, relaxation techniques, training, sports management, and tests.

Teachphysed.com—A Free Newsletter for Phys. Ed Teachers

http://teachphysed.com/

This site was created and is maintained by Ben Pirillo. It has wonderful resources—lesson plans, assessments, field day events, and a newsletter. Check out the Heart Obstacle Course that he created for a heart unit. The links to other P.E. sites are very comprehensive and add to the richness of this site. This is a great site with a personal touch.

Teachers.Net—Physical Education Lesson Plans

http://www.teachers.net/cgi-bin/lessons/sort.cgi?searchterm=Phys+ed

This physical education site is part of Teachers.Net lesson exchange. Teachers.Net offers lesson plans sorted by subject level and it allows users to search for, submit, or request a lesson.

P.E. Digest

http://www.pedigest.com/

Physical Education Digest has a new resource—the Library of Sport, Coaching, and Physical Education (LSCAPE). They have replaced their quarterly magazine with a website that provides hundreds of articles on sports, coaching, and physical education topics. Their resources can be easily viewed, downloaded, printed, or emailed. This is a fee-based website, but you might find its resources worth the annual subscription charge.

Health

Holiday Resources

Introduction

Schools have been working hard to promote the understanding of different cultures and lifestyles. Holidays provide an interesting way for students to look at what is important to people with cultural, religious, or ethnic differences. The first five resources are general in nature. They offer a wide spectrum of lesson plans and activities; the others are holiday specific. Also included are sites with folktales. Folktales are a big part of anyone's culture and traditions. It is fun for students to study the folktales of an area when they are also studying about the area's holidays and celebrations.

SUGGESTED activity

Have your students research Yahoo Kids Around the World—Holidays at **http://kids.yahoo.com/directory/Around-the-World/Holidays.** Research the holiday sites before you begin this project to make sure that the holidays you have chosen have sufficient information and graphics. Divide your students into pairs. Have each student pair research a certain holiday. Have one student be the online navigator, and the other can be the recorder, taking important notes about the holiday's traditions, history, and other fun facts. After their research is finished, have students create a poster or a multimedia presentation with information and pictures from the different links found at this website. Finally, have them present their projects to the class so that everyone can learn a little about different holidays and traditions.

Holidays

Holiday Resources (cont.)

General Holidays

Scholastic World Holiday Traditions

http://teacher.scholastic.com/holiday/factsfun.htm

Students can explore 21 different holiday traditions from around the world. An explanation and an interactive activity is provided for each holiday. This site gives students a broad base for understanding the range of holidays and celebrations that are celebrated worldwide.

Yahoo Kids—Around the World—Holidays

http://kids.yahoo.com/directory/Around-the-World/Holidays

This site, from the Yahoo Kids Directory, is a great place for kids to find out about holidays. It offers extensive resources, interactive and creative games, and activities.

Fact Monster—National Holidays

http://www.factmonster.com/ipka/A0882306.html

Fact Monster from Info Please provides an extensive link to holiday-related sites. It provides the calendar dates for major holidays and festivals for religious groups, and national holidays and festivals around the world. This is a good place for students to begin their research.

Crayola—Lesson Plan Search

http://www.crayola.com/educators/lessons/index.cfm

The lesson plans at this Crayola site were designed to show that communication not only involves language and the visual arts but also social studies, science, and math. Crayola offers engaging activities for students, related to topics that include countries and nations, culture, celebrations and holidays, folklore and stories, families, keepsakes, and native peoples. Your students will enjoy this fun-filled site.

Enchanted Learning—Symbols of the USA

http://www.enchantedlearning.com/history/us/symbols/

Enchanted Learning—National Holiday Crafts

http://www.enchantedlearning.com/crafts/

Enchanted Learning provides basic information, activities, and crafts for students. It is a good site for primary students to visit when they are working independently or at home.

Holidays

Holiday Resources (cont.)

Folktales and Folklore

American Folklore

http://www.americanfolklore.net/

This folklore site contains retellings of American folktales, Native American myths and legends, tall tales, weather folklore, and ghost stories from each of the 50 United States. Students can read about all sorts of famous characters like Paul Bunyan, Pecos Bill, and Daniel Boone.

Scholastic—Myths, Folktales, and Fairytales

http://teacher.scholastic.com/writewit/mff/

This site has stories from many authors. It is a rich resource for learning about myths, folktales, and fairytales, and writing in these genres. Students will see that each culture has its own response to similar situations that they make richer by details from its society and their environment. Students can read the folktales provided and then follow the help provided to write their own folktales and myths.

PBS—In Search of Myths and Heroes

http://www.pbs.org/mythsandheroes/

In this PBS series, Michael Wood goes in search of four of the world's most famous myths. He follows the path of the Queen of Sheba, searches for Shangri-La in Tibet, untangles the tales of King Arthur's Celtic Britain, and traces the trek of Jason who sought the Golden Fleece. The website that accompanies this PBS series has much to offer students learning about myths.

Aesop Fables to Read

http://www.umass.edu/aesop/fables.php

Professor Copper Giloth, of the University of Massachusetts, shares her students' illustrations of traditional Aesop's fables along with their retelling of the fables. Your students can review these fables and see how a computer can be used to create and share a story. Younger students will enjoy reading the traditional versions. Make sure you read the modern versions that Professor Giloth's students have written before your students read them. Then, decide if the stories are appropriate for your students and if your students are mature enough to understand them.

#50475—Must-See Websites for Busy Teachers

Holidays

Holiday Resources (cont.)

Specific Holidays

Scholastic—Culture and Change—Black History Month in America

http://teacher.scholastic.com/activities/bhistory/

Students can meet famous African Americans, listen to jazz music, publish their own writing, and explore history. They can use an interactive time line to learn more about African American history and the men and women who made a difference.

Lesson Plans Page—Black History Month

http://www.lessonplanspage.com/BlackHistoryMonth.htm

Lesson Plans Page has a number of links to sites with excellent lessons. They have an interdisciplinary 10-day unit that explores the secrets of the underground railroad.

Enchanted Learning—Activities and Crafts for President's Day

http://www.enchantedlearning.com/crafts/presidentsday/

President's Day craft projects are described for preschool, kindergarten, and elementary school children. They are great to use as homework activities. Most of this site is free to use, but if you want to print their materials, you will need to become a site member.

Lesson Plans—St. Patrick's Day

http://www.teach-nology.com/teachers/lesson_plans/holidays/stpats/

Whether it's graphing with Lucky Charms or making St. Patrick's Day snacks and food, using a writing prompt or singing songs, you will be pleased with the range of lesson plan ideas available at this site.

Holidays

Holiday Resources (cont.)

Specific Holidays (cont.)

Kid's Domain—St. Patrick's Day Crafts

http://www.kidsdomain.com/craft/_StPat.html

This site has great ideas, like creating a leprechaun catcher for St. Patrick's Day. Try some with your students to add a little fun to celebrating this special day.

Mexico for Kids about Mexico—Holidays and Traditions

http://www.elbalero.gob.mx/kids/about/html/home.html

This site was created by the president's office in Mexico. In the About Mexico section, there is information about holidays, myths and stories, traditions, recipes, music, and games. The brightness and variety of this site makes it worth visiting. You can choose to view the site in English, or if you want to give your students a challenge, have them view the Spanish version of the site.

Cinco de Mayo—Web Quest

http://www.zianet.com/cjcox/edutech4learning/cinco.html

Cinco de Mayo is not Mexican Independence Day, but it is an important date in the history of Mexico. This site explains the difference. It is geared to teach second–third grade students about the culture and traditions of Hispanic people.

Day for Mothers—Mother's Day

http://www.dayformothers.com/mothers-day-crafts/make-a-collage.html

This site has a little bit of everything. Have children explore and decide what Mother's Day is all about, what it might mean to them, and how they might honor their mothers and other females who have been important in their lives.

Holidays

#50475—Must-See Websites for Busy Teachers

Holiday Resources *(cont.)*

Specific Holidays *(cont.)*

Education World—Father's Day

http://www.education-world.com/holidays/archives/fathers_day.shtml

Education World offers resources, ideas for celebrating, craft projects, recipes, music, games and activities, and clip art. Check this site out for ideas to help your students celebrate their fathers or other male figures who have helped them in their lives.

About.com—Father's Day for Educators

http://k-6educators.about.com/library/bldadsday.htm

Use the lesson plans, writing activities, special projects, and other ideas for the classroom to find and plan a meaningful lesson for your class around the theme of Father's Day.

The New Colony: Planning for Independence—4th of July

http://score.rims.k12.ca.us/activity/indepday/

This site offers a great 4th of July simulation activity. Students can learn about how the leaders of the American colonies made it clear they were no longer part of England. Students will study the symbols they created—the flag, the anthem, the holidays, and the monuments. Then, they will separate their class from the other classes in the school, as the colonists did from England, and design their own class. They will make up symbols that will show that they are independent from the rest of the school. This activity is well described and is geared to the third grade but could be used by other grade levels too.

Education World—4th of July Lesson Plans and Activities

http://www.education-world.com/a_lesson/lesson069.shtml

This is a robust collection of 4th of July lesson plans and activities. There are Internet resources that include biographies, American documents, quizzes, and additional 4th of July sites.

Holidays

Holiday Resources [cont.]

Specific Holidays [cont.]

Kiddyhouse—Halloween

http://www.kiddyhouse.com/Themes/halloween/halloween.html

Teachers will find great resources to help them plan Halloween lessons. There are sections for stories, songs, poems, games, crafts, clip art, and Halloween facts and history.

Scholastics—The First Thanksgiving

http://teacher.scholastic.com/thanksgiving/

Students will learn how the Pilgrims reached America and lived to celebrate the first Thanksgiving.

Education World—Hanukkah

http://www.education-world.com/a_lesson/lesson040.shtml

Education World offers cross-curricular activities about Hanukkah. It also provides a review of related books.

The Teacher's Planet—Passover

http://www.teacherplanet.com/resource/passover.php

This site is an excellent resource for lesson plans and units, worksheets, clip art, and other resources relating to Passover. It also provides links to many other resources.

Lesson Plan Page—Easter

http://www.lessonplanspage.com/Easter.htm

This site offers great Easter-related lessons that focus on using eggs, chicks, and bunnies in areas such as language arts, math, and science.

Holiday Resources *(cont.)*

Specific Holidays *(cont.)*

A Colonial Christmas in Williamsburg

http://www.history.org/history/teaching/colxmas.cfm

Christmas is one of 12 areas that students can visit at this Colonial Williamsburg site to give them an insight into life in 18th-century America. This site has great American history resources to use with your students. They will enjoy its interactive nature.

North Pole.com

http://www.northpole.com/Overview/Teacher.html

This site offers some fun activities. They provide a variety of experiences for children. There are reading, writing, and math activities and games. The theme of the North Pole and Santa's Secret Village is very motivating for children. You will be amazed at how much this site has to offer. This is also a great site to share with parents.

Kwanzaa on the Net

http://www.holidays.net/kwanzaa/

This Kwanzaa link has information about the celebration, activities for families, and recipes, crafts, and greeting cards.

EdSelect—New Year's and Winter Activities

http://www.edselect.com/new_year%27s_activities.htm

A number of unique activities make this a worthwhile site to visit. Ticker Time, A Journey in Time, and Time Flies are examples of math-related activities that are very engaging and focus on real life. This site also includes many resources and lesson plans for Chinese New Year.

Holidays

Holiday Resources [cont.]

Specific Holidays [cont.]

Teacher Vision—Chinese New Year

http://www.teachervision.fen.com/chinese-new-year/china/6603.html

Check out Teacher Vision's Chinese New Year resources for ideas and resources. A membership is required to have full access to Teacher Vision. You may want to try a free trial membership to see if this site would be useful to you. They have excellent resources and a theme library. They also have printables, quizzes, worksheets, a reference section, language arts, mathematics, music, and art sections.

PBS—Martin Luther and Martin Luther King, Jr.—A Comparison

http://www.pbs.org/empires/martinluther/

This PBS special focuses on Martin Luther, a Protestant revolutionary whose belief in his faith overthrew the Catholic Church and reshaped Medieval Europe. Students can learn about a day in the life of a monk and read a comparison between him and Martin Luther King, Jr.

Bethany Roberts' Valentine Day Fun for Kids

http://www.bethanyroberts.com/Valentinefun.htm

Bethany Roberts has provided a great resource with Valentine jokes, games, tongue twisters, crafts, projects, and recipes. She also includes stories, poems and songs, fun printables, and links to many other Valentine Day resources and site. This site is a wonderful choice for all students and their families. Do not miss Bethany Roberts' big surprise. It is sure to bring a smile to your face.

1001 Postcards

http://www.postcards.org/

It is interesting to see the variety of themes that these postcards have. Besides the 4th of July and Canada Day, you can send a card for Funky Chicken Day, Ice Cream Day, or Teddy Bear Picnic Day. This is a fun site to use. Have your students try making their own online cards.

Lesson Plans and Teacher Resources

Introduction

The Web has made such a difference in the availability of materials and resources for educators. The ones included here are some of the very best. We do not want to list so many sites that you are unable to explore them all. The listings here provide lesson plans and curriculum ideas in general. Specific subject area website listings are presented in individual curriculum area sections.

When selecting technology materials for their classroom, teachers should check that these materials relate to the standards set by the International Society for Technology in Education and that they meet acceptable curriculum standards, too.

SUGGESTED activity

Review the ISTE/NETS standards for Educational Technology. Create a checklist of the standards. Assess what is currently being done in your classroom and your school, and what needs to be added. Set goals for yourself and your program. Many companies have excellent learning materials available for sale. They give prospective buyers an opportunity to review their materials by offering sample pages online. Before you buy materials, you should go to a company's website to check out the resources they offer. For example, visit Teacher Created Materials Publishing at **http://www.teachercreatedmaterials.com/estore/search** to review the products it offers. Select a curriculum area of interest to you and explore its available resources. Use the sample pages that are available for download to evaluate the usefulness of materials for your class. This way of shopping for learning and lesson plan materials should provide you with a more dependable and positive experience.

Lesson Plans and Teacher Resources [cont.]

Education and Technology Standards

McREL's Internet Connections

http://www.mcrel.org/standards-benchmarks/

McREL offers content standards and benchmarks for K–12 education in both search and browse formats. It offers links to lesson plans and other resources that are helpful for curriculum planning, including activities developed at McREL for specific benchmarks within their compendium. This is a highly respected resource. You will find excellent lesson plan ideas that relate directly to the needs of your classroom program.

ISTE—International Society for Technology in Education

http://www.iste.org/

Anyone involved with using technology and the Internet should become familiar with ISTE. Their mission is to "provide leadership and service to improve teaching and learning by advancing the effective use of technology in education." ISTE is the home of the National Educational Technology Standards (NETS), the Center for Applied Research in Educational Technology (CARET), and the National Educational Computing Conference (NECC). Check out their educational and curricular resources. The book resources at this site provide a good base for schools to use when planning their school's technology focus. Use this site to keep up on what is changing in the world of technology education.

NETS—National Educational Technology Standards

http://cnets.iste.org/

NETS—National Educational Technology Standards Project works to define standards for students, integrating curriculum technology, technology support, standards for student assessment, and evaluation of technology use. Make sure you review NETS Curriculum Standards, NETS for Students, and NETS for Teachers. Their resources provide an excellent way to evaluate and plan your school and classroom technology programs. Review their teacher technology standards to see how you measure up and how you might set goals for your personal technology development.

Lesson Plans and Teacher Resources [cont.]

Education and Technology Standards [cont.]

Profiles for Technology Literate Students

http://cnets.iste.org/students/s_profiles.html

National Educational Technology Standards for Students (NETS) describes its profiles with the following statement: "The Profiles for Technology Literate Students provide performance indicators describing the technology competence students should exhibit upon completion of the following grade ranges: Grades PreK–2, Grades 3–5, Grades 6–8, and Grades 9–12. These profiles are indicators of achievement at certain stages in PreK–12 education. They assume that technology skills are developed by coordinated activities that support learning throughout a student's education. These skills are to be introduced, reinforced, and finally mastered, and thus, integrated into an individual's personal learning and social framework. They represent essential, realistic, and attainable goals for lifelong learning and a productive citizenry." These profiles should be the basis of any district/school technology program. If you or your school is not familiar with these ISTE/NETS standards and profiles, perhaps plans could be made for a professional development day that focuses on this information.

NETS Standards for Teachers

http://cnets.iste.org/currstands/cstands-netst.html

This site from ISTE/NETS provides standards for assessing teacher technology knowledge, skills, and attitudes for applying technology in educational settings. All teachers should review these standards to assess their own performance. By doing this, teachers will know what their strengths are and in what areas they may need to do additional work.

Lesson Resources

National Education Association—Lesson Ideas

http://www.nea.org/lessons/index.htmlx

The National Education Association site's In the Classroom section has lesson ideas, classroom management suggestions, a Do the Right Thing link, a Works4Me, and a Dropout Prevention section. This site is great for new classroom teachers. By reviewing the experiences of others, you can see what you already thought you should do, and you can get ideas for what you can add to your program. This should help to make you feel more comfortable starting out.

Lesson Plans and Teacher Resources (cont.)

Lesson Resources (cont.)

AOL at School

http://www.aolatschool.com/

Built for primary, elementary, middle school, and high school classes, AOL@SCHOOL presents great links to K–12 educational content on the Internet. You can search their online database of educator-reviewed classroom materials to find teaching activities, lesson plans, learning games, tutorials, research, and multimedia resources. There are resource sections for both teachers and students.

Internet 4 Classrooms—K-12 Links

http://www.internet4classrooms.com/k12links.htm

This site has grouped its resources by Elementary Resources, Subject Area Resources, Instructional Resources, and General Resources. These subcategories provide a wonderful opportunity for teachers to search for useful materials they can use in their classrooms.

Internet 4 Classrooms—Online Practice Modules

http://www.internet4classrooms.com/on-line.htm

This site offers online lesson plans and instructions for popular software like *Word*, *PowerPoint, Excel, Inspiration*, and *Internet Explorer*. The plans and the instructions are for both the Windows and the Mac operating systems. These are easy to follow and use. Each link provides more resources as you begin to explore the site. There is something here for the beginner and the expert.

Internet 4 Classrooms—Daily Dose of the Web

http://www.internet4classrooms.com/daily_dose.htm

Have your students start each day with a visit to one of these Internet sections: Question of the Day, Subject Area, Quotation Source, Brain Teasers, and Interesting Trivia. Using these resources will provide a focus for your students when you are starting the day or while you work individually with students.

Lesson Plans and Teacher Resources [cont.]

Lesson Resources [cont.]

Kathy Schrock's Guide for Educators

http://school.discovery.com/schrockguide/

Kathy Schrock's Guide for Educators is part of Discovery Education—Discovery School.com. It is a categorized list of sites useful for curriculum and professional growth. Kathy Schrock's site includes Subject Access, Search Tools, Teacher Helpers, and Kathy's Picks. This site is updated often to include the best sites for teaching and learning. This site is well known and respected, and certainly one you should put at the top of your list for exploring.

Teacher Planet/Educators Network

http://www.teacherplanet.com

This site has much to offer teachers. More than 190,000 teachers have joined the Educators Network in the past three years. It focuses on the needs of teachers, particularly K–12 educators. Their goal is to help teachers save time and money by maximizing their online experience. All their sites are free to educators around the world. The Teacher Planet Lesson Plan section offers links to Lesson Planning Help, Lesson Plans Directories, and Lesson Plans for Subject Areas. It also has sections for themes, worksheets, teacher tools, rubrics, awards and certificates, quotes, jokes, and online degree opportunities.

K–12 Lesson Plans in the Yahoo! Directory

http://dir.yahoo.com/Education/k_12/teaching/lesson_plans/

Yahoo offers a collection of sites that offer lesson plans for teachers of kindergarten through high school. Some of Yahoo's subject areas are languages, literature, math, reading, science, social studies, and writing.

PBS Teacher Source

http://www.pbs.org/teachersource/

PBS Teacher Source includes more than 1,000 free lesson plans that are matched to standards, teacher guides, and online activities. You can explore these resources by subject or grade level, or with keywords. The site includes information about how teachers and media specialists can legally tape PBS shows for classroom use. Their site allows you to set up a free account and receive newsletters about upcoming PBS offerings, tailored to your local viewing area. There is also information about ordering PBS videos. Be sure to add this site to your bookmark/favorites list.

Lesson Plans and Teacher Resources [cont.]

Lesson Resources [cont.]

Thinkfinity/MarcoPolo

http://www.marcopolo-education.org/home.aspx

Thinkfinity is the Verizon Foundation's signature digital learning platform designed to improve educational and literacy achievement. It was developed from the foundation's education program formerly known as Verizon MarcoPolo, a comprehensive online resource for literacy. It provides no-cost, standards-based Internet content for K–12 teachers and classrooms. Its online resources include professionally developed lesson plans, classroom activities, materials to help with daily classroom planning, and powerful search engines.

AT & T Knowledge Network Explorer: Blue Web'n Homepage

http://www.kn.pacbell.com/wired/bluewebn/

Blue Web'n is an online library of 2,066 outstanding Internet sites categorized by subject, grade level, format-tools, references, lessons, hotlists, resources, tutorials, activities, and projects. You can browse by broad subject areas/content areas or specific subcategories/subject areas. You can even use their free tool, Filamentality, to build your own lessons and formats. Because technology, regulations, and funding opportunities change so quickly, it is helpful to have a reliable source for current information. The site presents general information about discounts and funding to help schools, libraries, and colleges explore technology possibilities so you can make informed decisions. They can direct you to sources for free network consulting and provide specific information about discount programs, like the California Teleconnect Fund and E-rate.

Apple Learning Interchange (ALI)

http://edcommunity.apple.com/ali/

The Apple Learning Interchange is a social network for educators. This exciting site introduces teachers and students to what is new in technology and education and helps them make using what is new a reality. The Apple Learning Interchange offers wonderful resources ranging from simple lesson ideas to in-depth curriculum units for K–12 educators. They also have a section for higher-education faculty and students. You can create a free account and gain access to a site for publishing and collaboration that is rich with movies, images, and sounds. You can also subscribe to RSS feeds that will alert you when new material of interest is added.

Lesson Plans and Teacher Resources [cont.]

Lesson Resources [cont.]

Teachers.net—Lessons

http://teachers.net/lessons/

This is the lesson plan section of Teachers.net. You can browse the Lesson Bank by grade level or subject area, or you can search using their keyword search engine. What makes this site so robust is that teachers can submit their own lesson ideas, or they can add their ideas to already existing lessons. For example, numerous teachers have provided ideas to the lesson plans for the letter W.

SchoolExpress

http://www.schoolexpress.com/

SchoolExpress.com is an educational website that furnishes a large number of free educational resources that can be used to help students practice different skills. There is a lot to explore at this site. They have activity sets and thematic unit sets, worksheets in categories that include handwriting, language arts, phonics, math, activities, and fun-time activities like daily treasure hunts. Your students can do self-graded math worksheets online, or you can print math worksheets with answer sheets. The site includes 20 online stories with colorful images and large type for young children, or you can download 30 children's reading e-books that include leveled readers and read-aloud books. You can also download more than 130 software programs including a PuzzleMaker generation tool and create awards online. Your children will also enjoy their 365 easy-to-use journal-writing worksheets.

Teaching Ideas for Primary Teachers

http://www.teachingideas.co.uk/

This United Kingdom site is an award–winning collection of hundreds of teaching ideas and activities that can be used in the primary classroom with worksheets that can be printed and photocopied. There are also some great ideas for math activities using Mathematics Worksheet Factory at **http://www.teachingideas.co.uk/Maths/Mathsws.htm**.

Top Teaching Resources

http://www.topteachingresources.com/

Top Teaching Resources provides a one-stop information source designed to help educators find high-quality curriculum electronic teaching resources. You can use this site to find suitable lessons plans, view up-to-date grants for teachers, get the latest educational news, and find ebay teaching resources.

Lesson Plans and Teacher Resources [cont.]

Lesson Resources [cont.]

Cool Teaching Lessons and Units

http://www.coollessons.org/coolunits.htm

This link is a treasure chest for teachers. It will save many hours of your time finding quality lesson plans and units. It is designed as a resource for K–12 teachers who want to find quality ready-made units and lessons for all subjects, or who wish to develop their own units. This site emphasizes student-engaged activities and lesson plans such as WebQuests, research, project-based learning modules, online projects, and ready-made units and lesson plans. You can use their cutting-edge unit formats to build your own units for your students. You can choose from engaged learning, WebQuests, and problem-based learning formats. You can also plan your students' evaluation by using their rubric and checklist resources.

Teachers Network

http://www.teachersnetwork.org/

This site contains links to hundreds of educational websites. You can search by keyword, subject, and grade; enjoy the latest educational news; find out about grants and online courses; and learn about current research and survey projects.

The Teacher's Corner—Teacher Resources and Lesson Plans

www.theteacherscorner.net/

Teacher's Corner offers free lesson plans, thematic units, seasonal items, bulletin board ideas, teacher resources, and printable worksheets. It also has a Teacher's Lounge with news, forums and contests, a Book Nook with children's, teen, and professional books and a message board.

LessonPlanZ.com—Lesson Plans and Lesson Plan Resources for Teaching

http://www.lessonplanz.com/

Lesson Plan Z has a searchable directory for teachers, containing thousands of lesson plans and lesson plan resources for all grades and subjects. It has a free newsletter with the latest updates, announcements, and featured site review. You can also have the newsletter delivered straight to your email inbox.

Lesson Plans and Teacher Resources [cont.]

Lesson Resources [cont.]

Internet Activities for Foreign Language Classes

http://www.clta.net/lessons/

This site offers Internet-based lesson plans that were created for foreign language classes by participants in the Technology Workshops of the California Foreign Language Project and the California Language Teachers Association. These plans include worksheets for the students to complete. You can print out the sheets, copy them, and distribute them to the students. The languages included are Spanish, French, German, Italian, Japanese, Chinese, and Latin.

Google Directory—Reference—Education—Directories

http://www.google.com/Top/Reference/Education/Directories/

Google has 24 directories that are related to education topics and issues. This is a good place to look to explore new areas of interest.

ECB Surf Report: Lesson Plans

http://explore.ecb.org/education/surf_report?subject=0

The Wisconsin Educational Communications Board (ECB) publishes a monthly guide to educational websites for teachers and students.

HotChalk

http://www.lessonplanspage.com/edulinks.html

The resources are limitless at this site. HotChalk is for teachers, students, and parents. Besides having incredible resources, you can use the site to post your homework online, share lesson plans, and manage your grade book online. There are thousands of schools across the country with access to HotChalk. Best of all, it does not cost anything to use.

Lesson Plans and Teacher Resources [cont.]

Lesson Resourcces [cont.]

SMART Boards

http://education.smarttech.com/ste/en-US/Ed+Resource/

Do you have a new SMART Board? Having new technology in the classroom can bring tremendous benefits to learners, but it can be scary for teachers who need to learn how to use it. At this site, you will find activities, programs, and training to help you get the most from your SMART products.

Using Electronic Whiteboards in Your Classroom

http://www.waukesha.k12.wi.us/WIT/SmartBoard/specificapps.htm

If you are fortunate enough to have a SMART Board in your classroom, this site will be useful to you. This site offers ideas for using electronic whiteboards—SMART Boards—in your classroom with profiles, ideas, lesson plans, and websites.

Language Arts and Literature Resources

Introduction

Teachers' efforts to assist their students with their reading and writing skills can be made easier and enhanced by using the incredible resources available on the Internet. The following language arts and literature sites have been divided into three categories: general, reading, and writing. This section will help teachers find sites to complement their language arts curriculum with writing practice, reading and writing resources, grammar, phonics, specific genre writing help, and fun interactive activities and games. The reading section offers sites for young children just learning how to read and sites for older children who are looking for reading material. Learning to read with online games and activities that incorporate memorable characters is advantageous for any student. The writing section has an array of activities ranging from writing workshops and step-by-step lessons to writing biographies and research papers. It also has grammar tutorials and lesson plans.

SUGGESTED activity

Review and organize your findings at these language arts sites. Before you begin your review, choose a topic that is relative to an area of your language arts curriculum that you would like to enhance. You may have a specific student need that you feel would benefit with additional resources or activities. Create a spreadsheet or table document to organize your search. Title your spreadsheet or table with the topic you are researching. For example, you might choose Grammar and Spelling Help and Activities as your topic. Next, create a reference for each of the sites that relate to your need. Make sure it includes the website name, its address, and a brief description of what is available at the site that you can use with your students. Organize your sites by the order in which you want to look at them. Select and review only a few sites at a time. Try to find something that you can start using right away.

Topic: Grammar

Grammar Blast Capitalization and Punctuation Game—2nd Grade Level
http://www.eduplace.com/kids/hme/k_5/quizzes/
This is a good game for capitalization and punctuation review. Students choose the correct answer from four choices. Have students work in pairs so they can discuss their choices.

Language Arts and Literature Resources (cont.)

General

National Council of English Teachers

http://www.ncte.org/

The National Council of English Teachers provides staff development information, teaching ideas, teacher chat, educational research articles, and great classroom resources. This site is important for all language arts and English teachers.

International Reading Association

http://www.ira.org/

The International Reading Association's Web page features literacy news, international literacy projects, reading research, and advocacy.

Web English Teacher

http://www.webenglishteacher.com/

Web English Teacher presents great resources: lesson plans, WebQuests, videos, biography, e-texts, criticism, jokes, puzzles, and classroom activities.

Schools of California Online Resources for Education (SCORE) Language Arts

http://www.sdcoe.k12.ca.us/score/cla.html

SCORE for Language Arts includes cyberguides: Web-based study units, which are based on books that are part of a language arts curriculum. SCORE also has a great activity center. The activities include graphic organizers, journaling, literature, and rubrics.

Davis School District—Secondary Language Arts

http://www.davis.k12.ut.us/curric/languagearts/links.html

This site has links to many of the topics and activities that a secondary language arts teacher needs. There are sites for reading, writing, speaking, media literacy, literature, research, grammar, vocabulary, poetry, Shakespeare, and professional resources.

Language Arts and Literature Resources (cont.)

General (cont.)

Internet 4 Learning—Language Arts Section

http://www.internet4classrooms.com/lang.htm

Internet 4 Learning provides a comprehensive list of language arts sites. It includes reading, comprehension, writing, and elements of language. It also has a Language Arts Skill Builder section and a Language Arts Assessment section.

Scholastic Online Learning Activities

http://teacher.scholastic.com/activities/

Scholastic Online has great resources that are organized into subject areas by grade. The Language Arts section includes content area reading, vocabulary, and more. Teacher guides will help you integrate activities into your curriculum.

British Broadcasting Company Schools—Learning Resources for Home and School

http://www.bbc.co.uk/schools/

This site has news stories, primary and secondary learning resources and great interactive learning materials. It offers many creative and engaging activities that you can use with your students.

Fact Monster—Reference Site

http://www.factmonster.com/index.html

Fact Monster comes from the Information Please Site. Its Reference Desk has an encyclopedia, time line, atlas, dictionary, almanac, and a homework center. This site is a good source for information and it has excellent word games for students.

Language Arts and Literature Resources (cont.)

Reading

Children's Literature Web Guide

http://www.acs.ucalgary.ca/~dkbrown/

The Children's Literature Web Guide has excellent resources related to books for children and young adults. Some of its sections include Authors on the Web, Stories on the Web, Readers' Theatre, Recommended Books, Journals and Book Reviews, Resources for Teachers, Parents, Storytellers, Writers and Illustrators, Research Guides and Indexes, Internet Book Discussion Groups, and Children's Literature Organizations on the Internet. Be sure to look at this site before you look at any other site.

Reading Rockets: Reading Comprehension and Language Arts Teaching

http://www.readingrockets.org/atoz

Reading Rockets offers strategies, lessons, and activities designed to help young children learn to read.

SCORE—Phonics Activities

http://www.sdcoe.k12.ca.us/score/Phonics_Link/classroom.html

This SCORE site provides teachers with a systematic framework for implementing phoneme awareness and phonics activities into grades K–3.

Internet Public Library—Reading Resources

http://www.ipl.org/kidspace/browse/rzn0000

The Reading Zone is a little like the fiction section at a public library. Students can find links to online stories and learn more about their favorite books and authors.

Learn to Read at Starfall

http://www.starfall.com/

This site is one of the best for interactive learning-to-read activities. It was designed for first grade but can also be used for Pre-K, kindergarten, and second grade.

Language Arts

Language Arts and Literature
Resources *(cont.)*

Reading *(cont.)*

Sadlier Oxford

http://www.sadlier-oxford.com/

Sadlier Oxford provides wonderful resources for teachers and students. This is their online catalog with products in areas of vocabulary, phonics, grammar, writing, and reading. They also provide activities that will provide practice for students needing more work on their skills and challenging activities for those students who need enrichment and advanced activities. The grade range for this site is Pre-K through sixth Grade.

EDUSCAPES—Literature Based Language Ladders

http://eduscapes.com/ladders/index.html

This is a site with excellent resources as well as easy-to-use lesson design help. Some of its areas include Themes and Literature Circles, Collaborative and Interactive Projects, Literature-Based WebQuests, Literacy across the Curriculum for Today and Tomorrow, Newberys and the Net, Caldecott Connections, and Fun with Favorites Ladders of Your Own.

EDUSCAPES—Literature Based WebQuests

http://eduscapes.com/ladders/themes/webquests.htm

This link at Eduscapes deals specifically with WebQuests. It provides links to previously created WebQuests as well as resources for creating your own WebQuests.

PBS Kids Learning Activities

http://pbskids.org/

There are activities, games, and music related to favorite PBS characters such as Arthur, Clifford, and the Berenstein Bears. They provide teacher guides for each character's books, and a parent link with great ideas to use at home.

Language Arts and Literature Resources (cont.)

Reading (cont.)

Jan Brett's Official Web Site

http://www.janbrett.com/

This site is both charming and inviting. There are nearly four thousand pages of activities and projects for children. Every student should have an opportunity to visit this site. It is a great way to enrich and motivate readers.

Clifford—Phonics Fun for Early Readers

http://teacher.scholastic.com/clifford1/index.htm

Students can read a story or play a game about Clifford at this Scholastic site. Early readers can practice important phonemic awareness and phonics skills.

Curious George

http://www.georgeworld.com/

All kids love Curious George. This link will give your students reading activities, games, and birthday ideas related to Curious George.

Seussville

http://randomhouse.com/seussville/

Seussville provides an exciting, engaging way for kids to work with Language Arts skills, particularly reading and writing. You will find Click and Play games, Print and Play games, a Quote Maker, and a Seussville Story Maker.

A-Z Teacher Stuff—Celebrate Dr. Seuss

http://www.atozteacherstuff.com/Themes/Dr__Seuss/

A-Z Teacher Stuff provides lesson plans with activity sheets and student handouts to use with many Dr. Seuss books. This site has great ideas and resources.

Language Arts and Literature
Resources [cont.]

Writing

Scholastic—Writing with Writers

http://teacher.scholastic.com/writewit/

At this site, students have a great opportunity to work with authors, editors, and illustrators in online workshops designed to help them further develop their writing skills. Folktales, mysteries, myths, news, poetry, speech, biographies, book review, and descriptive writing workshops are provided.

TIME for Kids Writing Ideas—Give Your Writing a Boost

http://www.timeforkids.com/TFK/hh/writeideas

TIME for Kids provides a Writer's Toolbox with a dictionary, thesaurus, homework helper, search tool, map finder, bibliography help, and clip art. The site also offers directions and writing tips for writing a compare-and-contrast essay, how-to article, news story, oral report, biography, book report, persuasive essay, business letter, personal narrative, and a research paper. If you work on any of these types of writing with your students, be sure to check out this site.

TIME for Kids: Writing Ideas and Rapid Research

http://www.timeforkids.com/TFK/hh/rr

TIME for Kids has a Writing Ideas and a Rapid Research section. These were designed to help students with their homework. Students can search their Rapid Research directory sections: Science, Language Arts, Social Studies, Math, Arts, and Research and Resources. They can get writing ideas and tips so that they can write great papers. You should also check out the TIME for Kids teachers section at **http://www.timeforkids.com/TFK/teachers**. TIME for Kids uses student reporters chosen by TFK and TIME editors to cover news, conduct interviews, and write reviews for TIME For Kids. If you have a talented student, you might like to recommend that he or she check out this opportunity.

Language Arts and Literature
Resources (cont.)

Writing (cont.)

PoetryTeachers.com—Giggle Poetry

http://www.poetryteachers.com/index.html

This site offers teaching ideas and ways to inspire your students to write different types of poetry. It has 11 categories of poetry, poems to read, and poetry theater scripts. Students will particularly enjoy all the fun activities and games.

Poetry Class—Kids' Poetry Sites

http://www.poetryclass.net/kids.htm

There are wonderful resources for teachers and students at this site. Sections include Poetry Lessons, A Fun Read, Places to Submit Poetry, Writing Tips, and Competitions.

RhymeZone

http://www.rhymezone.com/

RhymeZone offers a tool that students can use to find rhyming words for words they provide. This site can also find synonyms, definitions, antonyms and other word connections. It is a great tool for students.

FictionTeachers.com—Fiction Fun

http://www.fictionteachers.com/

This site has a section called Fiction Fun with great activities for students. Teachers can use the lesson plans with their exciting short story anthologies. This site has also created classroom theater scripts—plays that are based on their stories.

Scholastic's Mystery Writing with Joan Lowery Nixon

http://teacher.scholastic.com/writewit/mystery/

This learning activity helps students increase their skills in mystery writing by following the tips and suggestions from writer Joan Lowery Nixon. Using this site will provide your students with a fun way to learn about mystery writing and to try writing their own stories.

Language Arts and Literature Resources [cont.]

Writing [cont.]

Sherlockian

http://www.sherlockian.net/

This site is all things Sherlock. A great place for students to research and find interesting facts and stories related to Sherlock Holmes—it is great resource for a research project.

The Biography Maker

http://www.bham.wednet.edu/bio/biomaker.htm

The Bellingham Public School System provides a step-by-step lesson to help students in grades 4–8 write biographies. They have designed The Biography Maker to inspire lively storytelling and vivid writing so their readers will want to know more about the individual they are covering in their biography.

Read, Write, and Think Biographies—Creating Time Lines of a Life

http://www.readwritethink.org/lessons/lesson_view.asp?id=26

Third- to fifth-grade students can explore multiple sources to create a time line about the life of a particular person. Students can research and resolve potentially conflicting information about the individual they are researching. Students finish by developing an essay from their research material. A Biography Selection, a Rationale Sheet, and a Time Line Tool are provided at this site.

Internet Public Library for Teen—A+ Research Writing

http://www.ipl.org/div/aplus/

This site offers a step-by-step guide to writing a research paper. It is a good site for students to use when they are writing a research paper.

Scholastic—Write It: Essay

http://teacher.scholastic.com/writeit/essay/index.htm

Using Write It, students can find step-by-step help through the writing process and see how master writers work. This site is related to essay writing in particular, but others sections relate to poetry, short fiction, memoirs, humor, and journalism writing. Students can chat with fellow writers, publish their own work, and create portfolios.

Language Arts and Literature Resources [cont.]

Writing [cont.]

Principles of Composition

http://grammar.ccc.commnet.edu/grammar/composition/composition.htm

This site has three sections: The Writing Process, Structural Considerations, and Patterns of Composition. Each has a drop-down menu for specific help and information. This site allows for personalization, so it is a good choice for students with different needs.

A Guide to Grammar and Writing

http://grammar.ccc.commnet.edu/grammar/

This Guide to Grammar and Writing provides tutorials at the word, sentence, and paragraph levels. It also has sections for grammar help with essays, research papers, quizzes, and *PowerPoint* presentations.

Grammar Blast

http://www.eduplace.com/kids/hme/k_5/quizzes/

Houghton Mifflin presents grammar-related games and activities for grades K–5.

Wacky Web Tales

http://www.eduplace.com/tales/index.html

Wacky Web Tales is like Mad Libs. Students enter words that are specific parts of speech to make a wacky story. This is a fun way to practice parts of speech with students.

National Spelling Bee

http://www.spellingbee.com/

This site provides information about the National Spelling Bee. It supplies a year's worth of spelling and vocabulary activities, tips, and lessons to help prepare students.

Language Arts and Literature Resources [cont.]

Writing [cont.]

Education World—Spice up Your Spelling Lessons

http://www.education-world.com/a_lesson/lesson282.shtml

Education World provides five lesson plan ideas to help students learn spelling. It includes a weekly spelling plan, spelling resources, and games for different grade levels.

Children's Lit.Com—Meet Authors and Illustrators

http://www.childrenslit.com/f_mai.htm

This site has a link to author page collections, and hundreds of authors and illustrators.

Literacy Connections: Readers Theater

http://www.literacyconnections.com/ReadersTheater.php

This website provides guides for implementing reader's theater, a book list with reader's theater scripts, and reader's theater scripts online.

The Old Farmer's Almanac

http://www.almanac.com/

Since 1792, *The Old Farmer's Almanac* has published useful information. This site will provide students with much of the information that is available in the book version of *The Old Farmer's Almanac*.

The Old Farmer's Almanac for Kids

http://www.almanac4kids.com/

This is the kid's version of *The Old Farmer's Almanac*. Its topics of interest are geared toward younger students. Best of all, students can personalize the almanac to suit their needs.

Math Resources

Introduction

The following websites are organized by math topics that relate to the needs of students from kindergarten through grade 12. There are general math websites that include lesson plans, worksheets, math manipulatives, and games, as well as specific websites that focus on algebra-, calculus-, and geometry-related topics. These sites can be used as an enrichment or extension to your existing math program, or they can be used to help students who are having difficulty with specific areas of math. Many of the sites will provide an opportunity for your students to practice their math skills in an interactive setting. With the sites in Math Tools and Calculators, you can create worksheets for your students, or your students can use online graphing calculators and a currency converter. Also provided are sites that will entertain and motivate your students with challenging math games and activities. Look at these sites to find ones that will help you add to your math curriculum. Use the lesson plans or have your students work online to improve their math skills.

SUGGESTED activity

Identify several specific problems your students are having with math. Review the descriptions of the sites that have been provided. Select sites that include interactive activities that you can use with your students. Create a list that pairs the name of the site with the specific math help and activities it offers. Match your list of activities to students who need specific help. Have your students try the sites and then have them report to you about their experiences and whether the sites helped them. Update your list and then share it along with site descriptions and its reviews with parents. You can use these activities for extra at-home practice too, particularly if you have limited time and computer resources available in your classroom.

Math Resources (cont.)

General

AAA Math

http://www.aaaMath.com/

This site has hundreds of pages of math lessons for grades K–8. Each page explains a math topic and offers interactive practice with immediate feedback. They also have great math challenge games.

Ask Dr. Math

http://Mathforum.org/dr.Math/

Math students and their teachers can search Dr. Math's archive that is arranged by level and topic, or they can ask him specific math questions.

Internet 4 Classrooms—Math

http://www.internet4classrooms.com/grade_level_help.htm

This is a wonderful site with math resources and practice activities by subject and grade level. Its interactive sites are for kindergarten through eighth grade.

Math Forum

http://Mathforum.org/library/

This is an Internet-based mathematics library. It is divided into Math Topics, Math Resources, Education/Teacher Topics, and Education Levels. The site's search engine can be used to find specific links or to browse for a math topic of interest.

McREL—Mid Continent Center for Research and Learning—Mathematics

http://www.mcrel.org/lesson-plans/Math/index.asp

McREL, the standards people, have a Mathematics Lesson Plan Library that has an excellent collection of lesson plans, downloadable resources, and tools for use in the classroom. Their Web-based resources are helpful for curriculum planning.

Math Resources [cont.]

General [cont.]

A+ Math

http://www.aplusMath.com/

This website helps students improve their Math skills. It offers a Game Room with games like Matho. Students can work online or create and print their own set of flashcards or worksheets. They can use a Homework Helper to check their homework too.

Mathematic Lessons that Are Fun

http://Math.rice.edu/~lanius/Lessons/index.html

This site offers 23 great topics with lessons aimed at specific levels from Pre-K through college. Some of their online activities are interactive.

Superkids—Math Tools

http://www.superkids.com/aweb/tools/Math/

Make your math drill sheets at SuperKids. You select the type of problem and the maximum and minimum numbers to be used, and their site tool creates a worksheet to your specifications. This site can help you provide individualized worksheets for your students so they can all be challenged and receive practice that is customized to their specific needs.

Awesome Library for Students—Math

http://www.awesomelibrary.org/Mathg.html

The Awesome Library's K–12 Math resources are organized under the following topics: elementary, middle, high school, and college math, lesson plans and standards.

Cool Math

http://www.coolMath.com/

This site offers tutorials, practice, and challenge activities for every age. Its sections include math games, algebra, free online games and puzzles, and continuing education. Challenge your students to try the different Cool Math Thinking Games found here. These games provide a good alternative to the usual format of a math class.

General [cont.]

Web Math

http://www.webMath.com/

WebMath has been programmed to not only give students an answer to a math problem, but to also show students how to do it. Their topics include Math for Everyone, General Math, K–8 Math, Algebra, Plots and Geometry, and Trigonometry and Calculus. This site allows students to evaluate their progress and work on any problems they are having.

National Council of Teachers of Mathematics: Illuminations—Marco Polo

http://illuminations.nctm.org/

NCTM's library has 92 online activities that help make math more interactive. They provide more than 500 lessons for Pre-K–12 Math educators, and hundreds of exemplary online resources.

Interactive Websites—Math

http://jc-schools.net/tutorials/interactive.htm#Math

Jefferson County School District offers an extensive listing of interactive math sites. Interactive Websites provides standards-based, cross-curricular Web resources that have been designed to enhance online learning opportunities. These sites interact with the user through a text-based or graphical user interface.

SCORE Mathematics Lessons

http://score.kings.k12.ca.us/lessons.html

These lessons have been written for teachers and students in California. Its contents and links reflect California's Mathematics Standards and National Council of Teachers of Mathematics Standards.

National Library of Virtual Manipulatives for Interactive Mathematics

http://matti.usu.edu/nlvm/nav/vlibrary.html

This site is amazing. It contains a library of interactive, Web-based virtual manipulatives, and concept tutorials. This site is fun and engaging for student and gives them an opportunity to experiment with mathematical concepts.

Math Resources (cont.)

General (cont.)

PBS: Math

http://www.pbs.org/teachersource/Math.htm

Teacher Source provides an accurate and easily searchable database of PBS lesson plans, offline activities, and online interactives for teachers. Materials can be searched by grade level, topic area, or keywords. The activities are connected to high-interest topics and familiar PBS themes, adding extra motivation for student participation.

Curious Math

http://www.curiousMath.com/

Fun and fascinating math tricks and trivia can be found at CuriousMath.com. This is a great site for students who have a keen interest in math.

The Abacus: The Art of Calculating with Beads

http://www.ee.ryerson.ca:8080/~elf/abacus/

The abacus was one of the first calculating tools used by humans. This site provides an interesting history of the abacus and its use. An interactive abacus with a built-in tutor for counting, addition, and subtraction is provided.

A Fractals Unit for Elementary and Middle School Students

http://Math.rice.edu/~lanius/frac/

This fractals site is for kids. It will help them understand the math properties of these colorful, beautiful, and often odd pictures. Every lesson has a printable version for classroom use.

Math Resources [cont.]

Algebra

Math.Com—Algebra

http://www.Math.com/practice/Algebra.html

This is a site with sections on the language of algebra, the basics of algebra, equations and inequalities, and graphing equations and inequalities. Each section has a unit quiz and there is a worksheet generator provided as well.

Algebra Help

http://algebrahelp.com/

Algebrahelp.com is a collection of lessons, calculators, and worksheets created to assist students and teachers of algebra.

Quick Math

http://www.quickMath.com/

QuickMath is an automated service for answering common math problems over the Internet. It has an online calculator that solves equations and does all sorts of algebra and calculus problems instantly and automatically.

Purple Math

http://www.purpleMath.com/modules/index.htm

This highly respected site includes more than 150 algebra lessons with explanations, demonstrations, and solution examples. The areas covered include preliminary topics, beginning algebra topics, intermediate and advanced algebra topics, and an appendix that includes a section of placement tests and advice on buying a calculator.

SOS Math

http://www.sosMath.com/algebra/algebra.html

S.O.S. MATH is a perfect study site for high school and college students. It offers students homework help, explanations of topics to refresh their memory, and test preparation practice. Its CyberExam is a place for students to take practice tests, midterm exams, and final exams.

Math Resources (cont.)

Algebra (cont.)

Go Math

http://www.goMath.com/

Go Math has challenging and stimulating puzzles for high school students. Topics include algebra and geometry solutions, formulas, virtual physics, and SAT math.

Calculus

Calculus.org

http://calculus.org/

Calculus.org offers an extensive list of resources for the calculus student and teacher. Included are step-by-step solutions, calculus animations, classroom demonstrations, tips on test preparations and sample exams, and links to a great number of calculus sites.

Karl's Calculus Tutor

http://www.karlscalculus.org/

If a student is having difficulty with a calculus topic, they can select a topic, look at the text, and then follow along with the worked-out problems to learn how to do similar ones on his or her own. There is also remedial coverage of algebra topics, number systems, exponentials, logs, trig functions, and trigonometry if students are in need of review.

Calculus Help.com

http://www.calculus-help.com/

Michael Kelly offers multimedia tutorials with clear explanations of limits, continuity, and basic derivatives. He also offers interactive cheat sheets that contain the formulas a student needs for Calculus I and II.

Math

Math Resources [cont.]

Geometry

Math.Com—Geometry

http://www.Math.com/homeworkhelp/Geometry.html

Sections included at this site include Geometry Building Blocks, Polygons, Relations and Sizes, Three-Dimensional Figures, and Tables and Formulas.

Yahoo Education—Homework Help—Geometry

http://education.yahoo.com/homework_help/Math_help/geometry

At Yahoo Education—Geometry there are hundreds of practice problems with step-by-step explanations. This site is for geometry, but other math areas are included at the main site.

Euclid's Elements

http://aleph0.clarku.edu/~djoyce/java/elements/toc.html

Euclid's Elements form one of the most influential works of science. This site uses JAVA applets to illustrate all of Euclid's 13 Books—even those in the last three books on solid geometry that are three-dimensional.

Math Challenges

Kid's Place Brain Teasers

http://www.eduplace.com/Math/brain/

These weekly brainteaser math puzzles will provide a great challenge for your students. They are arranged by grade level and include hints in case help is needed.

Fun Brain Kids Center

http://www.funbrain.com/kidscenter.html

This is a fun, interactive site for students. The games can be individualized and students can compete with themselves or with others. This is a great site for your reluctant math student.

Math

Math Resources (cont.)

Math Challenges (cont.)

White House Math Challenge Archive

http://www.whitehouse.gov/kids/Math/archive-elm.html

The White House Math Challenge provides math questions for elementary, middle, and high school students. There is an Open Challenge section for students too.

BBC—Learning Resources for Home and School—The Math File Game Show

http://www.bbc.co.uk/education/Mathsfile/index.shtml

Join ancient mathematicians for online games and printable worksheets covering numbers, algebra, shapes, space, and measures. Check out the BBC Home and School home page for other math activities too at **http://www.bbc.co.uk/schools/**.

McGraw Hill Math Resources

http://www.mhschool.com/math/2003/student/index.html

McGraw Hill has provided Web-based activities and lesson plans with printable worksheets for a variety of subject areas. Make sure students try the Math Fact Dash game found on the Math section's main page.

Math Tools and Calculators

Superkids Math Worksheet Creator

http://www.superkids.com/aweb/tools/math/

Make your own worksheets. Select the type of problem from 15 different areas of math, the maximum and minimum numbers in the problems, and then click for your worksheet. You can also print an answer sheet for the worksheet that was generated. It is great to be able to create custom worksheets.

Currency Converter

http://www.oanda.com/converter/classic

The FXConverter (Foreign Exchange Currency Converter) is a multilingual currency converter with up-to-date exchange rates for 164 currencies. Whether you are studying other cultures, you or your students are planning a trip, or you just want your students to have practice working with this real-life skill, this site is a good one to use.

Math Tools and Calculators [cont.]

Web Graphing.com

http://www.webgraphing.com/

Web Graphing has online graphing calculators—function graphing, equation plotting, multiple equation plotting, inequality graphing, and 3D graphing. You can copy publication quality graphs into your tests, and your students can check their homework and get solutions to graphing related problems.

Roman Numeral Conversion

http://www.ivtechstudios.com/roman/

Students can type in an Arabic numeral up to 4,000 and get the Roman numeral equivalent.

Math.Com Library

http://www.Math.com/students/references.html

Students can find formulas at this site and graph and plot their data. They can also use the math dictionaries, study math history, and find out about famous mathematicians at the biography and quote resource sections. This site also links to sites with great ideas for Science Fair Math projects.

Money and Banking

Young Investor—Fleet Kids

http://www.younginvestor.com/

The Fleet Kids' site has a great collection of interactive games to help students with their math skills and become better prepared to manage money. Students can play the games on their own to practice their math skills, or play for their school to earn technology-related awards.

Math Resources ^[cont.]

Money and Banking [cont.]

U.S. Treasury for Kids

http://www.ustreas.gov/kids/

At this site, students can learn about the Mint, the Bureau of Printing and Engraving, and savings bonds. It has enjoyable games to play and interesting activities and information.

The Mint

http://www.themint.org/

The Mint contains printable lesson plans and online resources that teach the basics of personal money management and economics for grades 6–12. Students can learn "How to Be a Millionaire" and play the Real World Credit Card Game or other interactive games and quizzes. It also includes a dictionary of financial terms.

Wise Pockets for Kids

http://www.umsl.edu/~wpockets/index.html

This site provides an interactive game that teaches about money management. It is a great place for kids, parents, and teachers.

Escape from Knab

http://www.escapefromknab.com/

This simulation takes place on the planet Knab. If students make the right financial decisions, they will get back to Earth. This great activity includes lesson plans and activity sheets for classroom use.

Change Maker

http://www.funbrain.com/cashreg/index.html

At this site, students figure out how much change they should get back—both bills and coins—when they pay for something. International currencies for the United States, Canada, Mexico, Great Britain, and Australia are available. If a student's answer is correct, the change is added to his or her piggy bank. If the answer is wrong, the correct amount is subtracted from the piggy bank.

Professional Teacher Organizations

Introduction

Professional organizations help educators stay in touch with others in their field and stay current with what is happening in education. Teachers are often isolated in their classrooms on a day-to-day basis, so having an organization for support and professional growth is very important. The following list of professional organizations relate to many different areas of education.

SUGGESTED activity

Look through the following list to see if one or more of these organizations would be valuable to your professional development. See if your school would support your membership. As you are looking through these sites, make a list of the organizations that you think may be of interest to other staff members at your school. Check to see if anyone at your school belongs to or is interested in belonging to any of these organizations. Share your list and provide the websites so others can check them out too.

Professional Teacher Organizations [cont.]

Organizations

National Education Association (NEA)

http://www.nea.org/index.html

The National Education Association is the nation's largest professional employee organization. It is committed to advancing the cause of public education. The NEA's 3.2 million members work at every level of education—from preschool to university graduate programs. NEA is a volunteer-based organization supported by a network of staff at the local, state, and national levels. At the local level, more than 14,000 affiliate organizations are involved in a variety of activities that the local members decide on. These activities may include raising funds for scholarship programs, conducting professional workshops on issues that affect faculty and school support staff, or bargaining contracts for school district employees.

American Federation of Teachers (AFA)

http://www.aft.org/

The American Federation of Teachers is a 940,000-member union of public and professional employees, including public and private school teachers, paraprofessionals and school-related personnel, higher education faculty and professionals, employees of state and local governments, nurses, and other health professionals.

United Federation of Teachers (UFT)

http://www.uft.org/

The United Federation of Teachers, with more than 125,000 members, is the largest union in the United States. It represents more than 68,000 teachers and 16,000 classroom paraprofessionals. The union also includes a Retired Teachers Chapter of more than 32,000 members. This organization deals with many issues relevant to teachers and their working environment.

Organizations *(cont.)*

American Association of University Women (AAUW)

http://www.aauw.org/

The American Association of University Women dates back to 1881. It promotes education and equity for women and girls through research, fellowships, and grants. They are also very politically active, working to promote women, voter education, and support for sex-discrimination lawsuits. If you are interested in getting involved with women's issues and helping promote their causes, then take a look at this site.

The National Association of Student Assistance Professionals (NASAP)

http://www.nasap.org/

The National Association of Student Assistance Professionals advocates high standards for their professionals and continuing development of their services. They promote student achievement and academic success, and a healthy, safe, and drug-free lifestyle. This association was founded in 1987 by professionals who were concerned about the problems of student substance abuse, violence, and academic underachievement.

American Association of School Administrators (AASA)

http://www.aasa.org/

The American Association of School Administrators was founded in 1865. It is a professional organization for over 16,500 educational leaders across North America and in many other countries.

National Association of Elementary School Principals (NAESP)

http://www.naesp.org/

The National Association of Elementary School Principals offers professional development training programs, regional and national conferences, and periodicals, including the award-winning *Principal* magazine, which reports on the latest research along with practical advice. NAESP also offers comprehensive legal assistance, salary and contract review, and services for students, including the American Student Council Association.

Professional Organizations

Professional Teacher Organizations [cont.]

Organizations [cont.]

National Association of Secondary School Principals (NASSP)

http://www.principals.org/s_nassp/index.asp

The National Association of Secondary School Principals serves all administrators in middle school and high school education. This website contains education news and information for parents, principals, and aspiring principals. They also support student activities that include the National Honor Society, National Junior Honor Society, American Technology Honor Society, National Association of Student Councils, National Association of Student Activities Advisors, the National Alliance of High Schools and the National Alliance of Middle Level Schools.

American Council on Education (ACE)

http://www.acenet.edu

Founded in 1918, the American Council on Education is an organization that supports higher education. ACE deals with higher education issues and looks to positively influence public policy through advocacy, research, and program initiatives.

The National Rural Education Association (NREA)

http://www.nrea.net/

The National Rural Education Association is the oldest established national organization of its kind. It traces its origins back to 1907 when it was founded as the Department of Rural Education. If you teach in a rural environment, and want to connect with other rural educators, then check out this site.

National Association of State Universities and Land-Grant Colleges (NASULGC)

http://www.nasulgc.org/

The NASULGC is a voluntary, nonprofit association of public universities, land-grant institutions, and many state university systems. It has member campuses in all 50 states and the U.S. territories.

Professional Organizations

Organizations [cont.]

Council for American Private Education (CAPE)

http://www.capenet.org/

The Council for American Private Education (CAPE) is a coalition of national organizations and state affiliates that serve private elementary and secondary schools. They have an excellent section that reviews the benefits of a private school education and a number of publications related to different private education programs, like those for children with disabilities. This site is an excellent resource for prospective parents who are considering enrolling their children in a private school environment.

National Council for Private School Accreditation (NCPSA)

http://www.ncpsa.org/

The National Council for Private School Accreditation was established in 1993 to serve as an accrediting association for private school accrediting agencies. They serve preschool, elementary, and secondary private schools.

Association of Christian Schools International

http://www.acsi.org/

The Association of Christian Schools International serves thousands of Christian schools around the world.

National Alliance of Black School Educators

http://www.nabse.org/

The National Alliance of Black School Educators is a network of African American educators dedicated to improving educational accomplishments of African American youth.

Association for Experiential Education (AEE)

http://www.aee.org/

The Association for Experiential Education is a nonprofit, professional membership association dedicated to experiential education and the students, educators, and practitioners who follow its philosophy. The organization connects educators in practical ways so that they have access to research, publications, and resources. Its members want to increase the recognition of experiential education worldwide, and raise the quality and performance of experiential programs with their accreditation program.

Professional Organizations

Professional Teacher Organizations [cont.]

Organizations [cont.]

American Library Association (ALA)

http://www.ala.org/

The American Library Association is the oldest, largest, and most influential library association in the world. For more than a century, it has been a leader in defending intellectual freedom and promoting the highest quality library and information services.

International Reading Association (IRA)

http://www.reading.org/

The International Reading Association is the world's leading organization of literacy professionals. Its goal is to "teach the world to read." The organization provides members with professional-development resources that include local, regional, national, and international workshops and conferences. If you are involved with teaching reading, you should check out the resources available through this organization.

American Literacy Council (ALC)

http://www.americanliteracy.com/

First organized in 1876, The American Literacy Council is an institution dedicated to "literacy research, publication, and the dissemination of literacy information and strategies for the improvement of literacy in English-speaking countries."

International Society for Technology in Education (ISTE)

http://www.iste.org/

The International Society for Technology in Education is an organization that focuses on the use of technology in Pre-K–12 educational programs and teacher education. ISTE represents more than 85,000 professionals worldwide. They support members with information and networking opportunities. It is home to the National Educational Technology Standards (NETS), and the Center for Applied Research in Educational Technology (CARET). ISTE hosts the annual National Educational Computing Conference (NECC). This conference provides exceptional technology resources and training for teachers and administrators.

National Council for Teachers of Mathematics (NCTM)

http://www.nctm.org/

With more than 110,000 members, the National Council for Teachers of Mathematics is the largest nonprofit professional association of mathematics educators in the world.

Professional Teacher Organizations (cont.)

Organizations (cont.)

National Science Teachers Association (NSTA)

http://www.nsta.org/

The National Science Teachers Association was founded in 1944. It is the largest organization in the world committed to promoting excellence and innovation in science teaching and learning.

American Educational Research Association (AERA)

http://www.aera.net

The American Educational Research Association was founded in 1916. The AERA is an international professional organization with the primary goal of advancing educational research and its practical application. Its 25,000 members are educators, administrators, directors of research, persons working with testing or evaluation in federal, state, and local agencies, counselors, evaluators, graduate students, and behavioral scientists.

National Council of Teachers of English (NCTE)

http://www.ncte.org/

The National Council of Teachers of English is the world's largest subject-matter educational association. NCTE has 90,000 members with subscribers in the United States and other countries. It is devoted to improving the teaching of English and Language Arts at all levels of education.

Teachers of English to Students of Other Languages (TESOL)

http://www.tesol.org/

Teachers of English to Students of Other Languages is an association of English as a second language teachers. TESOL membership connects teachers with an international group of teachers, educators, and researchers involved in the profession.

American Council on the Teaching of Foreign Languages (ACTFL)

http://www.actfl.org/

American Council on the Teaching of Foreign Languages is dedicated to the improvement and expansion of the teaching and learning of all languages at all levels of instruction.

Professional Organizations

Organizations [cont.]

National Council for Geographic Education

http://www.ncge.org/

The National Council for Geographic Education works to enhance the status and quality of geography teaching and learning. It promotes the importance and value of geographic education. It offers resources and opportunities for geographic educators with respect to their knowledge of content, techniques, and learning processes.

National Council for the Social Studies (NCSS)

http://www.ncss.org/

Founded in 1921, the National Council for the Social Studies has grown to be the largest association in the country devoted solely to social studies education. It involves and supports educators by advocating for social studies education. With members in all the 50 states, the District of Columbia, and 69 foreign countries, the NCSS serves as an umbrella organization for elementary, secondary, and college teachers of history, geography, economics, political science, sociology, psychology, anthropology, and law-related education.

National Art Education Association (NAEA)

http://www.naea-reston.org/

The National Art Education Association is an educational organization that promotes art education through professional development, service, advancement of knowledge, and leadership.

American Alliance for Health, Physical Education, Recreation, and Dance (AAHPERD)

http://www.aahperd.org

The American Alliance for Health, Physical Education, Recreation, and Dance is the largest organization of professionals supporting and assisting those involved in physical education, leisure, fitness, dance, health promotion, education, and all specialties related to achieving a healthy lifestyle.

Professional Organizations

Professional Teacher Organizations *(cont.)*

Organizations *(cont.)*

Council for Basic Education

http://www.c-b-e.org

The Council for Basic Education promotes high academic standards for all students by supporting efforts to strengthen the curriculum in traditional academic subjects and improve teacher quality.

Association for Childhood Education—International

http://www.acei.org/

The mission of the Association for Childhood Education International (ACEI) is to promote and support, in the global community, the optimal education and development of children from birth through early adolescence, and to influence the professional growth of educators and the efforts of others who are committed to the needs of children in a changing society.

North American Montessori Teachers' Association (NAMTA)

http://www.montessori-namta.org/

The North American Montessori Teachers' Association is a membership organization open to parents, teachers, and others interested in Montessori education. NAMTA provides publications, audiovisual collections, electronic communications, conferences, research, and service projects throughout North America and the world.

National Head Start Association

http://www.nhsa.org/

The National Head Start Association is a private membership organization dedicated exclusively to meeting the needs of Head Start children and their families. It represents more than 1 million children, 200,000 staff, and 2,700 Head Start programs in the United States. The association provides support for the entire Head Start community by advocating for policies that strengthen services to Head Start children and their families; providing extensive training and professional development to Head Start staff; and developing and disseminating research, information, and resources that enrich Head Start program delivery.

Professional Organizations

Professional Teacher Organizations

Organizations (cont.)

Council for Exceptional Children (CEC)

http://www.cec.sped.org/

The Council for Exceptional Children is the largest international professional organization dedicated to improving educational outcomes for students with disabilities and the gifted. CEC advocates for appropriate governmental policies, sets professional standards, provides professional development, advocates for newly and historically underserved individuals with exceptionalities, and helps professionals obtain the resources necessary for providing effective services and programs.

Center for Accessible Technology

http://www.cforat.org/

The Center for Accessible Technology provides access to computers for people with disabilities so they can succeed in school, find and keep jobs, and use the Internet and email.

American Psychological Association (APA)

http://www.apa.org/

Based in Washington, D.C., the American Psychological Association (APA) is a scientific and professional organization that represents psychologists. With 148,000 members, the APA is the largest association of psychologists worldwide. The goals of the American Psychological Association are to advance psychology as a science and profession and to promote health, education, and human welfare.

The Association for Supervision and Curriculum Development (ASCD)

http://www.ascd.org/index.html

The Association for Supervision and Curriculum Development is a highly respected association of educators whose goal is to advocate policies and share practices that will help all learners achieve success. Founded in 1943, the Association for Supervision and Curriculum Development is a nonprofit, nonpartisan organization that represents 175,000 educators from more than 135 countries and 58 affiliates. Their members span the entire profession of educators—superintendents, supervisors, principals, teachers, professors of education, and school board members.

Professional Organizations

Professional Teacher Organizations [cont.]

Organizations [cont.]

Association for Career and Technical Education (ACTE)

http://www.acteonline.org

The Association for Career and Technical Education is dedicated to the advancement of education programs that prepare youth and adults for careers. The ACTE Lesson Plan Library has many lesson plans submitted by educators in the field. Its lesson plans are grouped by career clusters and grade levels. This site is an excellent resource for all teachers.

Association of American Universities

www.aau.edu/

Founded in 1900, the Association of American Universities helps research-intensive universities in the United States and Canada focus on issues such as funding for research, research policy issues, graduate and undergraduate education, and developing national policy positions.

National School Boards Association (NSBA)

http://www.nsba.org/

The National School Boards Association is a federation of state school board associations. Check their map to find the resources and programs that are available for each state. The NSBA and its members represent 95,000 local school board members who are "dedicated to educating every child to his or her fullest potential and committed to leadership for student achievement." The National School Boards Association is an advocate for public education, an important force for achieving equity and excellence in public education, and a vehicle for empowering communities on behalf of education.

PTO Today

http://www.ptotoday.com/

PTO Today is dedicated to helping parent teacher groups like PTOs and PTAs help their schools with expert ideas, articles, and information on relevant issues like fund-raising, family nights, back-to-school, and playground building. PTO Today also offers PTO Management Tools, a great resource for parents. This is a great site to suggest to your on-campus parent group.

Professional Organizations

Professional Teacher Organizations [cont.]

Organizations [cont.]

Project Appleseed

http://www.projectappleseed.org/

The mission of Project Appleseed, the National Campaign for Public School Improvement, is to leave no parent behind. Project Appleseed is a digital network that helps parents and educators across the nation look for effective parental involvement. Their goal is to organize America's 50 million public school parents to volunteer a minimum of 10 hours each year to improve the nation's 15,000 public school districts and 90,000 public schools.

United States Student Association (USSA)

http://www.usstudents.org/

The United States Student Association (USSA) is the country's oldest and largest national student organization, representing millions of students. Founded in 1947, USSA is a recognized voice for students on Capitol Hill, in the White House, and in the Department of Education.

Scholarship and Continuing Education Opportunities

Teach for America

http://www.teachforamerica.org/

Teach for America is a corps of recent college graduates of all majors and cultural backgrounds who commit two years to teach in under-resourced urban and rural public schools.

Japan Fulbright Memorial Fund Teacher Program

http://www.fulbrightmemorialfund.jp/teacher_program.html

Japan Fulbright Memorial Fund Teacher Program annually provides 400 American primary and secondary school teachers and administrators with opportunities for professional development. They offer short-term study visits to Japan with the opportunity to earn academic credits. JFMF's program is designed to provide educators with firsthand opportunities to experience Japanese culture and education through school visits, interactions with teachers and students, seminars, and exchange and host programs. Check out their website to learn more about their application process.

Professional Organizations

Professional Teacher Organizations [cont.]

Scholarship and Continuing Education Opportunities [cont.]

P.E.O. International

http://www.peointernational.org

P.E.O. International promotes education opportunities for women through chapters throughout the United States and Canada. P.E.O. has five international projects: Educational Loan Fund, Cottey College, International Peace Scholarship Fund, Program for Continuing Education, and Scholar Awards. The P.E.O. is based in Des Moines, Iowa.

Milken Family Foundation

http://www.mff.org

The purpose of the Milken Family Foundation is to discover and advance inventive and effective ways of helping people help themselves. This foundation is committed to strengthening the education profession by recognizing and rewarding outstanding educators through expanding their professional leadership and policy influence. They want to attract, develop, and retain the best teaching talent, encourage learning as a lifelong process, and build vibrant communities by involving people of all ages in programs that contribute to the revitalization of the community and to the well-being of its residents.

International Education Financial Aid

http://www.iefa.org/

IEFA is one of the resources available for financial aid, college scholarships, and grant information for students in the United States and international students wishing to study abroad. At this site, you will find a comprehensive college scholarship search and grant listing, plus international student loan programs and other information to promote study abroad.

MacArthur Foundation

http://www.macfdn.org

The MacArthur Fellows Program awards five-year, unrestricted fellowships to individuals who show exceptional merit and promise of continued creative work. It is limited to U.S. citizens and other residents of the United States. Their Program on Human and Community Development addresses issues in the United States that include community and economic development; housing, with a focus on affordable rental housing; juvenile justice reform; and education, with an interest in how digital media impacts learning. Their opportunities are worth reviewing if you are involved with any of their areas of interest.

Professional Organizations

Professional Teacher Organizations [cont.]

Scholarship and Continuing Education Opportunities [cont.]

FinAid—The Smart Guide to Financial Aid

http://www.finaid.org/

FinAid was established in the fall of 1994 as a public service. This award-winning site has grown into one of the most comprehensive sources of student financial aid information, advice, and tools. Access to FinAid is free for all users. It has earned a reputation in the educational community as one of the best websites of its kind. It is comprehensive and informative. Many think FinAid should be the first stop on the Web for students looking to finance their educations.

FastWeb

http://www.fastweb.com/

FastWeb is another source of local scholarships, national scholarships, and college-specific scholarships. Students and teachers can search and compare detailed college profiles, including college scholarships. More than 15,500 high schools and 3,500 colleges recommend this site. Students can also look for internships in their fields, find part-time job openings near their homes or schools, and learn tips for success in their careers. Students can input information and FastWeb will search its database for scholarships, grants, or other relevant opportunities.

FastAID—College and University Scholarships

http://www.fastaid.com/

FastAID offers a free scholarship search. It is one of the largest private sector scholarship databases in the world. It is similar to FastWeb.

College and University Scholarships (CAUS)

http://collegeuniversityscholarships.com/

College and University Scholarships is another funding source database that is similar to FastWeb and FastAID. They provide information about the differences between scholarships, grants, and loans and help students define their special areas of interest or ability so that narrowing down the search process is easier.

Science Resources

Introduction

The following science sites were chosen with two things in mind. They are intended to provide teachers with links to classroom resources and information and to provide students with interactive experiences and exciting materials that will help motivate them to become more interested in studying and learning more about science.

SUGGESTED activity

Dissections are a part of many middle school and high school biology programs. Visit either Cow Eye Dissection at **http://www.exploratorium.edu/learning_studio/cow_eye/** or Net Frog at **http://frog.edschool.virgina.edu/**. (In the Life Science section, there are also sites for a sheep's brain dissection and a virtual fetal pig dissection.) At Cow Eye Dissection, your students can either watch a real-life dissection of a cow eye, learn about eyes, or receive instructions to do their own dissections. At Net Frog, your students can watch a step-by-step dissection of a frog with audio and video clips. If you want students to prepare for a dissection in the classroom, they can visit these sites to prepare and see the process and what needs to be done during lab time. Or, they can learn about anatomy by seeing the virtual online dissections.

Science Resources (cont.)

General Reference

Scholastic Science Lesson Plans

http://teacher.scholastic.com/

The teacher center at Scholastic has incredible resources. Search for science in general or for the specific science topics or ideas that you need.

The Yuckiest Site on the Internet

http://www.yucky.com/

All kids love yucky. If you have students who want learn some strange stuff, then send them to this site for yucky science information.

Bill Nye—Science Nye's Labs Online

http://www.billnye.com/billnye.html

Bill Nye the Science Guy developed this site. It includes episode guides, great hands-on experiments, science information and resources, questions of the week, and e-cards.

Center for Innovation in Engineering and Science Education

http://www.k12Science.org/currichome.html

Center for Innovation in Engineering and Science Education sponsors and designs projects that teachers can use to enhance their science curricula and have students become involved in online science projects.

✗ Internet4Classrooms—Virtual Field Trips

http://www.internet4classrooms.com/vft.htm

This site offers links to field trips of all sorts, from museums to a farm, plus tips for creating your own virtual field trips. Look them over and find ones that will enhance your science program.

Science Resources (cont.)

General Reference (cont.)

⅄ Scholastic—Science Internet Field Trips

http://teacher.scholastic.com/fieldtrp/Science.htm

An Internet field trip is a trip that takes place online at a website. With these field trips, Scholastic directs students through topics in life science, earth and space science, physical science, technology, and the history of science. Each Internet Field Trip highlights websites that serve to enrich the study of a specific curriculum theme or topic.

Ask Eric Science Lesson Plans

http://www.eduref.org/cgi-bin/lessons.cgi/Science

This site offers lesson plans for 12 areas of science. They include standards, references, complete directions, student handouts, and additional resources and references.

Busy Teacher's Web Site K–12

http://www.ceismc.gatech.edu/busyt

The goal of this site is to provide teachers with direct source materials, lesson plans, and classroom activities. The lesson plans includes several science categories.

⅄ Yahoo! Kids—Science and Nature

http://kids.yahoo.com/directory/Science-and-Nature

Yahooligans has become Yahoo! Kids. This new format is not as user-friendly as the old format, but it does have good resources.

Center for Innovation in Engineering and Science Education—Ask an Expert

http://www.k12Science.org/askanexpert.html

CIESE has an extensive list by subject of science-related Ask an Expert sites. This link is a good site for students wishing to contact an engineering or science expert.

Science

Science Resources (cont.)

General Reference (cont.)

Pitsco's Ask an Expert

http://www.askanexpert.com/

This site connects students with hundreds of real-world experts. Most of the experts have excellent websites with a wealth of information in their areas of expertise.

Chemistry

Chem 4 Kids

http://www.chem4kids.com/index.html

Students can learn about the states of matter, periodic table, structure of atoms, formulas and symbols, and reactions at this site. A glossary and summary quizzes are also included.

Delights of Chemistry

http://www.chem.leeds.ac.uk/delights/

There are more than 40 chemistry demonstrations, stunning chemistry movies, and more than 160 chemistry photos at this site. Safety considerations are included.

Atoms Family

http://www.miamisci.org/af/sln/

Students will love this site. The Atoms Family is a Science Learning Network resource based on The Atoms Family exhibit on display at The Miami Museum of Science.

Comic Book Periodic Table

http://www.uky.edu/Projects/Chemcomics/

This site shares pages in real comic books that reference elements of the periodic table. This format adds interest for students and hopefully a visual connection that will help them remember fact about the elements of the periodic table.

Science Resources [cont.]

Chemistry [cont.]

Chemistry Quiz Activities, Problems, Exercises and Worksheets

http://www.syvum.com/squizzes/chem/

This site provides quizzes and activities to help students with a variety of topics from their chemistry curriculum. They provide background information on specific chemistry topics and several quiz options for assessment.

Creative Chemistry

http://www.creative-chemistry.org.uk/

This site includes question sheets, practical guides, full-color worksheets, teaching notes, chemistry puzzles, interactive quizzes, and molecular models to help you with your chemistry program.

(Life Science)

Biology 4 Kids

http://www.biology4kids.com/index.html

This site provides information on cell structure, cell function, microorganisms, plants, vertebrates, invertebrates, animal systems, and other life science topics. Biology 4 Kids has wonderful illustrations and simple-to-understand explanations of the basics of each of the topics they present. A glossary and summary quizzes are also included.

Body Works Games

http://www.Scienceworld.ca/teachers_outreach/play_online/bw_games.htm

The Body Works site at Science World in Vancouver, British Columbia, offers interactive games that help younger students learn more about how their bodies work.

Michelangelo—Microscopic Views of Life

http://www.pbrc.hawaii.edu/microangela/index.html

Come explore familiar and unexpected views of the microscopic world with colorized images from electron microscopes at the University of Hawaii. These images are not only interesting, but they are also spectacular.

Science Resources (cont.)

Life Science (cont.)

Human Anatomy Online

http://www.innerbody.com/index.html

Each topic at Human Anatomy Online has animations, graphics, and descriptive links. It is interactive and an ideal reference site for students about the anatomy of the human body.

Biology Quiz Activities, Problems, Exercises and Worksheets

http://www.syvum.com/squizzes/biology/

This site provides quizzes and activities to help students with a variety of topics from their biology curriculum. They provide background information on specific biology topics and several quiz options for assessment.

Animal Bytes

http://www.seaworld.org/animal-info/animal-bytes/index.htm

Sea World's Animal Bytes is a collection of one-page fact sheets specifically designed to provide information about many of the special creatures found in the animal kingdom. Sea World offers additional resources for teachers and students too. These fact sheets are a great resource for student reports and presentations.

Bat Conservation International

http://www.batcon.org/

This site offers information about bats. It has the largest collection of bat photos in the world. You will find activities like crossword puzzles, crafts, quizzes, and e-cards at this site.

National Geographic

http://www.nationalgeographic.com/index.html

National Geographic has so much to offer. It is hard to explore this site without being distracted. Be sure you check out the Educators' section, the Kids' section, and the Magazine section. Their magazines offer excellent resources for your classroom and for kids and their parents to explore at home. Check out *National Geographic Kids*, *Little Kids*, and *National Geographic in the Classroom: Explorer,* and *Young Explorer* magazines.

#50475—Must-See Websites for Busy Teachers

Science Resources (cont.)

Life Science (cont.)

World Wildlife Fund

http://www.worldwildlife.org

World Wildlife Fund (WWF) offers opportunities to learn more about endangered species. Students can use a powerful search tool to discover where species live or explore wild places to find out what species live there.

Ace on the Case: Secrets@Sea

http://www.secretsatsea.org/

Ace on the Case: Secrets@Sea is a curriculum-based adventure story for grades 4–7. This engaging website game complements ocean-theme units of study, teaching concepts in ocean science such as ocean food webs, tides, currents, and mapping skills.

United States Fish and Wildlife Service—Endangered Species Program.

http://endangered.fws.gov/

This site from the United States Fish and Wildlife Service's Endangered Species Program demonstrates how loss of habitat and ecosystems can lead to a decline in biodiversity, and how the Endangered Species Act helps prevent extinction. They have resources for students at the Kids' Corner.

Cow Eye Dissection

http://www.exploratorium.edu/learning_studio/cow_eye/

This site provides a step-by-step online dissection of a cow eye. Students can watch online, learn about eyes, and download instructions to use with their dissection.

Net Frog

http://frog.edschool.virginia.edu/

Net Frog guides a student through a frog dissection as practice before, or instead of, an actual dissection. Excellent learning resources for students and teachers are also provided.

Science Resources (cont.)

Life Science (cont.)

Sheep's Brain Dissection

http://www.exploratorium.edu/memory/braindissection/

This site presents a discussion of the relationship between the brain and memory. By dissecting the brain of a sheep, students can see where memory processes take place in the brain. Because a sheep's brain and our brains are very similar, they can relate what they learn to human brains and memory.

Virtual Fetal Pig Dissection

http://www.whitman.edu/biology/vpd/main.html

This site provides an excellent learning tool that uses Shockwave to display interactive photos related to dissecting a fetal pig and learning about the pig's different body systems.

Virtual Cat Dissection

http://bio.bd.psu.edu/cat/

This site offers great photos with appropriately labeled parts to help make an actual dissection easier to do. It helps students learn about the internal body systems of a cat before they do a dissection.

Natural History Museums, Zoos, and Science Center Resources

TryScience.org

http://www.tryScience.org/

TryScience.org is a gateway to science and technology centers worldwide. Content is added regularly to their sections. The TryScience Teacher's section includes a wealth of resources to help teachers integrate science center resources into their classroom activities.

American Zoo and Aquarium Association

http://www.aza.org/

There are great resources here. Check out their A-Z index and their Kids and Families sections. The Wild Educator's Resource Guide is a great source of zoo and aquarium-based activities developed by AZA and Disney's *The Wild*. All of the activities are based on National Science Education Standards and are geared to grades 2–5.

Science

Science Resources [cont.]

Natural History Museums, Zoos, and Science Center Resources [cont.]

Smithsonian National Zoological Park

http://nationalzoo.si.edu/default.cfm

The National Zoo is an interactive site with sections for educators, kids, families, and scientists. Their photos and cams are great classroom resources.

Smithsonian—Students—A Place for Kids to Explore, Discover, and Learn

http://www.smithsonianeducation.org/students/index.html

The Smithsonian offers a great site for students. It has a New and Cool section, Favorites, and a Games and Activities section. This site is perfect for small-group computer activities.

Smithsonian Institution—National Science Resource Center—Curriculum Resources

http://www.nsrconline.org/curriculum_resources/index.html

The National Science Resource Center offers leadership development for school districts, professional development for teachers, science curriculum for K–8 students, and internships for high school and college students.

Exploratorium—Museum of Science, Art, and Human Perception

http://nsdl.org/resource

This is a great collection of interesting science sites. Thorough site descriptions make it easy to find activities and information. Check out the Animals and Plants section and the Education section. Make sure your students explore the Kids section. It is a great spot with animal information, crafts, recipes, and experiments.

San Diego Zoo

http://www.sandiegozoo.org/

This delightful site includes a teacher section with curriculum guides, classroom kits, activities, and a kids section with experiments and crafts linked to science content.

Science Resources [cont.]

Natural History Museums, Zoos, and Science Center Resources [cont.]

St. Louis Zoo

http://www.stlzoo.org/education/

The St. Louis Zoo is world famous. It has more than 5,000 animals from more than 700 different species. It has great teacher resources, lesson plans, and student activities. Students can even create their own virtual zoo.

Sea World—Just for Teachers

http://www.seaworld.org/just-for-teachers/index.htm

Sea World's lesson plans and activities are organized by grade level, and teacher guides are downloadable. Their resources provide excellent in-class reading and research material.

The Natural History Museum—London

http://www.nhm.ac.uk/index.html

The Natural History Museum is one of the most respected museums in the world. Its online offerings are first class. Students will love their activities.

Physical Science

Amusement Park Physics

http://www.learner.org/exhibits/parkphysics/

In Amusement Park Physics, students find out how the laws of physics affect amusement park ride design. They can design a roller coaster. If they plan it carefully and it passes a safety inspection, they can also experiment with bumper-car collisions. It is all great fun.

PBS—Build a Bridge

http://www.pbs.org/wgbh/nova/bridge/build.html

NOVA sponsors this site. Participants study bridge structures and determine the strengths and weaknesses of each type of bridge before playing an interactive bridge building game.

Science Resources (cont.)

Physical Science (cont.)

PBS—Building Big

http://www.pbs.org/wgbh/buildingbig/index.html

This site is a great addition to a bridge building science unit. Students can explore what it takes to build big structures like bridges, domes, skyscrapers, dams, and tunnels.

Internet 4 Classrooms—Physical Science

http://www.internet4classrooms.com/eoc_physci.htm

This site includes tutorials, interactive activities, and test practice for the following units: Force and Motion, Structure and Properties of Matter, Interactions of Matter, and Energy.

Physics Quiz Activities, Problems, Exercises, and Worksheets

http://www.syvum.com/squizzes/physics/

This site offers theory and quiz activities related to basic physics curriculum themes. They include matter, motion, force, pressure, work and energy, heat and changes in matter, light, sound, magnets, and electricity. This site is a good resource for students to use for review or for you to use for pre-unit assessment.

Science Fairs and Inventions

Internet Public Library—Science Fair Project Resource Guide

http://www.ipl.org/div/kidspace/projectguide

If your students need help getting started on a science fair project, you can have them visit this site to learn about the scientific method and the steps to coming up with a hypothesis. It also guides them through the process of choosing a topic by providing links to ideas and projects. Also important to good execution are the links for completing and displaying your project.

Science Fair Central

http://school.discovery.com/Sciencefaircentral/

This site offers comprehensive resources for creating a science fair project, a handbook, a question-and-answer section, tip sheets, and links to related sites and books.

Science

Science Resources [cont.]

Science Fairs and Inventions [cont.]

All Science Fair Projects

http://www.all-Science-fair-projects.com/

This is a great site for students to explore. They have a well-designed search engine to help students find information. They have hundreds of ideas for every science topic.

Edison National Historic Site

http://www.nps.gov/edis/home.htm

This site will provide your students with an opportunity to explore the life and work of Thomas A. Edison. There are great lessons to learn from Edison about hard work, creative genius, methodical research, practical design, and manufacturing.

Enchanted Learning—Inventors and Inventions

http://www.enchantedlearning.com/inventors/

The Enchanted Learning site has great Science resources for the K–3 learner. Its Inventors and Inventions section has short descriptions on hundreds of inventors and inventions. This is a great place for younger students to learn about famous people in science.

Inventions at About.Com

http://inventors.about.com/

About.com offers a search engine that presents a well-organized list of links. The Lesson Plan section has lesson plans for teaching about invention and inventors, experiments about inventing, information about inventions made by kids, and other science lesson plans for grades K–12. It also has contests for kids' inventions.

Invent America

http://www.inventamerica.org/

Invent America is a K–8 education program that helps children develop creative-thinking and problem-solving skills through a fun, unique, and proven learning tool—inventing. Check this site for ideas and information about their yearly competitions.

Science Resources (cont.)

Space Science

NASA for Kids

http://www.nasa.gov/audience/forkids/home/index.html

NASA for Students

http://www.nasa.gov/audience/forstudents/k-4/home/index.html

NASA's Quest—Ongoing Challenges and Projects

http://quest.arc.nasa.gov/

Where better to learn about space than through the resources offered by NASA? Each of these sites focuses on different age groups and topics. Use these sites to follow NASA's Space Missions and life on the International Space Center. Their photos of space, the planets, and other bodies in the universe are interesting and beautiful. Have students participate in their online activities and connect with their space experts—their astronauts and engineers.

Weather

Weather Classroom

http://www.weatherclassroom.com

This site has sections for teachers, students, and parents. Students create their own interactive weather forecast, become an intern at the Safeside Severe Weather Center, or go behind the scenes to explore a weather channel studio or do backyard weather observations. Their activities are interactive, educational, and great fun.

The Weather Channel

http://www.weather.com/

The Weather Channel has wonderful resources such as the ability to put a local weather forecast on your computer's desktop. Students can find local weather reports for thousands of cities and up-to-date maps for outdoor activities, health and safety, and weather details.

National Oceanic and Atmospheric Administration's—National Weather Service

http://www.weather.gov/education.php

NOAA provides websites with information about weather education for teachers, students, and a playtime for kids. It includes classroom resources and activities.

Science

Searching the Web

Introduction

The Web is so large that it is impossible to find what you are looking for without a search engine. Search engines are organized in two ways. The first allows you to search using keywords, and the second by looking at categories in a directory. For example, if you were looking for information about American presidents, you might try a word search using the keywords *American* and *presidents,* or you might go to a search engine's directory and find a category related to the information about American presidents for which you are looking. Keyword searches work well when you are looking for specific information, and directories work well when you are looking for information or ideas about a topic in general.

The Internet is an enormous and constantly changing medium, making it difficult for any single engine to scour the entire Web. Metasearch engines search multiple engines. This means that instead of getting the best results one search engine has to offer, you can get the best combined results from a variety of engines. Metasearch engines use industry-leading engines like Google, Yahoo, Search, MSN, Ask.com, About, and LookSmart. Using metasearch technology, a metasearch engine takes results from the leading search engines, eliminates the duplicates and delivers a comprehensive set of results. You benefit by obtaining a quicker, more accurate set of results for your inquiry. The two metasearch engines listed also provide multimedia results including images, audio, video, news, and local information.

SUGGESTED activity

Try exploring one search engine in depth. Google is a great one because it has so many features. Did you know that Google has more than 20 different types of search services, including searches for images, sounds, videos, and news? They also have an image storage application, and a variety of language applications. Google also has show and share services, services to use with your mobile devices, and ways to make your computer work better. Use Google's services at **http://www.google.com/intl/en/options/index.html**.

Searching the Web

Basic Search Engines

Google

http://www.google.com/

This popular search engine is probably the most widely used of all search engines. If you have not used it, you should check it out. It is especially popular with students.

Google's Directory of Searchable Categories

http://directory.google.com/

Google's directory has many categories to choose from. If you go to Kids and Teens and then School Time, you can find sites for specific subject areas, along with reference tools.

Yahoo

http://search.yahoo.com/

Visit About Yahoo Search at **http://tools.search.yahoo.com/about/forsearchers.html** to get specifics about all that is available at Yahoo, another popular search engine.

Yahoo! Kids

http://kids.yahoo.com/index

The old favorite, Yahooligans, has been changed to Yahoo! Kids. While the look is a little different, and it is not as easy to find educational materials in their Kids directory, it is still a good website. It features an easy-to-use search engine and directory with educational resources in all the subject areas. It also has many other sections—Games, Music, Movies, T.V., Jokes, Sports, Animals, Ask Earl, News, References, Homework Help, and a Study Zone.

Searching the Web (cont.)

Basic Search Engines (cont.)

AlltheWeb

http://www.alltheweb.com/

AlltheWeb is linked to Yahoo. Its index includes billions of Web pages, as well as tens of millions of PDF and *MS Word* files. You can search any or all of its categories: the Web, News, Pictures, Video, and Audio. Yahoo frequently scans the entire Web to ensure that its content is fresh and it has no broken links. It offers a variety of specialized search tools and advanced search features, and supports searching in 36 different languages. Their news search—provided by Yahoo—offers up-to-the-minute news from thousands of news sources all across the globe, with hundreds of stories indexed every minute. Their image, audio, and video searches include hundreds of millions of multimedia files.

KidsClick

http://www.kidsclick.org

KidsClick was created for kids by librarians. It offers a search engine and lists about 5,000 websites grouped in various categories in a directory. Some of its 15 categories include Facts and References, Weird and Mysterious, Religion and Mythology, Reading, Writing Speaking, Science, Sports and Recreation, and Geography, History, and Biography.

ALA—American Library Association Great Web Sites for Kids

http://www.ala.org/greatsites

This is an organized directory of sites selected by members of the American Library Association, using rigorous evaluation guidelines to assure high-quality content. Searches can be directed to age-appropriate materials for Pre-K, elementary, and middle school students.

Awesome Library

http://www.awesomelibrary.org/

The Awesome Library has taken more than 14,000 sites and classified them into a directory for teachers, kids, teens, parents, librarians, and college students. You can either browse the directory or search specifically for the information you want.

Ask.com

http://about.ask.com/

Jeeves is gone but the site remains an excellent search engine. It also has images, a map feature, news, and blogs.

Searching the Web (cont.)

Basic Search Engines (cont.)

Ask for Kids

http://www.askforkids.com/

Jeeves is gone here too! The revised site still has a Search Engine, News Resources, Reference and Study Help and a Fun and Games section. Even without Jeeves, this is still a good site for students to use.

Net Trekker

http://www.nettrekker.com

NetTrekker, a commercial site, is a new Internet search engine specifically designed for students and their parents. NetTrekker home delivers more than 180,000 websites, all reviewed, rated, and approved by teachers so parents can be confident that their children receive search results that are safe, pornography free, and on target, time after time.

Educational Search Engines

Education World

http://www.education-world.com/

Education World has created a site on the Internet for educators. Teachers can share ideas, and find lesson plans and research materials. Education World resources include a search engine for educational websites only. It also has lesson plans, practical information for educators, information on how to integrate technology in the classroom, articles written by education experts, employment listings, and much more. This site is easy to use, and it is a good bookmark choice for every educator.

The Educator's Reference Desk

http://www.eduref.org/

The Educator's Reference Desk provides high-quality resources and services to the education community. The individuals from the Information Institute of Syracuse, who produced AskERIC, the Gateway to Educational Materials, and the Virtual Reference Desk, have created the Educator's Reference Desk. It offers great educational resources—more than 2,000 lesson plans, 3,000 links to online education information, and 200 archived question responses.

Searching the Web [cont.]

Educational Search Engines [cont.]

ERIC—Educational Resource Information Centers

http://www.eric.ed.gov/

The Educational Resource Information Center's database provides free access to more than 1.2 million bibliographic records of journal articles and other education-related materials. When available, it includes links to full text. The U.S. Department of Education and the Institute of Education Sciences sponsor ERIC.

Metasearch Engines

Web Crawler

http://www.webcrawler.com/

WebCrawler is one of the most popular metasearch engines. It brings users the top search results from Google, Yahoo, Windows Live, Ask.com, About.com, MIVA, LookSmart, and other popular search engines. WebCrawler provides multimedia results including images, audio, video, news, and local information.

Dogpile

http://www.dogpile.com/

The inspiration for Dogpile came when its founders noticed that different search engines often return different results for the same search words. The more engines they searched, the more results they found. To capture this idea, the founders borrowed a sports term used to describe players piling on top of one another in celebration—Dogpile. Dogpile offers searches in the following categories: Web, Images, Audio, Video, News, Yellow Pages, and White Pages. Once the results are retrieved, the metasearch technology used by Dogpile goes to work removing duplicates and analyzing the results to help ensure that the best results top the list. Check out their Tools and Tips for help. It includes Arfie's Special Search Tools and Tips, Frequently Asked Questions, and Helpful Search Links.

Searching the Web—Techniques and Lesson Plans

Safe Kids—Safety on the Internet

http://www.safekids.com/

Safe Kids has a search engine to help you find information about safety on the Internet. The site provides a guide to keeping kids safe on the Internet while they are being productive and having fun. They have suggestions for parents and ideas for safety in chat rooms, on MySpace, and for safe blogging.

Searching the Web [cont.]

Searching the Web—Techniques and Lesson Plans [cont.]

FourNets for Better Searching

http://webquest.sdsu.edu/searching/fournets.htm

FourNets for Better Searching is a WebQuest activity geared to helping students learn a system for searching the popular search engine Google. The biggest problem people have with search engines is that they are too good! You can type in a word and within a fraction of a second, you will have too many sites to look at. Many of the sites will not be exactly what you were after, and you will have to spend a lot of time sorting through the sites to eliminate those that are not quite right. The FourNets for Better Searching activity helps searchers learn how to use Google's Advanced Search form located at **http://www.google.com/advanced_search** so they can be more precise about the words they choose when they are searching.

Web Search Strategies

http://www.learnwebskills.com/search/main.html

Because the Web is not indexed in any standard manner, finding information can be difficult. Without a clear search strategy, using a search engine is like wandering aimlessly in the stacks of a library trying to find a particular book. The tutorial available at this site presents easy-to-follow strategies for using search engines and subject directories to find what you need on the World Wide Web.

Searching the Internet

http://www.coollessons.org/search.html

This site offers a short lesson on searching the Internet. It presents simple ways to search using advanced techniques that use quotation marks, include and exclude (+ and –), lowercase, wild card, and Boolean search techniques.

Locating and Evaluating Information on the Internet

http://www.wam.umd.edu/~toh/search/

Locating and Evaluating Information on the Internet is another good Web page that offers information and practice searches to teach some of the skills necessary for good and efficient searching of the Web. It is well worth a visit to learn new skills or refresh your memory about some techniques you may have forgotten to use.

Social Studies

Introduction

The following social studies sites are amazing. There is so much valuable information offered here that it is almost impossible to think about getting to it all. Exploring these sites will enrich your curriculum and provide hours of enjoyment and fun for you and your students.

SUGGESTED activity

Again as with the other sections in this book, start by narrowing your site reviews. Enlist the help of others you work with to search too. As you find great sites, add them to your list and begin sharing them with your students. Remember, you only need to start with one site to engage your students and have them want to use the Internet to learn about the world around them and its history.

Have your students review history/geography sites and then have them create a directory of the sites they visited with reviews that they can share with one another. They can do a paper-type report or create a *PowerPoint* slide show to share their experiences about a particular site. To make their reviews available to others, consider creating a website review page and putting it on a class website that students can use to guide their Internet experiences.

Social Studies [cont.]

American History and Geography

Discovery School—U.S. History Lessons

http://school.discovery.com/lessonplans/ushis.html

This Discovery School—U.S. History site has lesson plans for K–fifth, sixth–eighth, and ninth–twelfth grade that include interesting topics, standards-based lesson plans, and a glossary of terms and standards for evaluating.

Teachnology—The Online Teacher Resource for U.S. History

http://www.teach-nology.com/teachers/lesson_plans/history/us_history/

Teachnology offers general sites and topic specific sections for American Presidents, Civil War, Black History Month, Elections and Voting, and States of America.

First Gov for Kids—History

http://www.kids.gov/k_history.htm

First Gov for Kids—Geography

http://www.kids.gov/k_geography.htm

These sites offer great resources for students and classroom teachers. There are links to many well-known sites for history and geography.

Whitehouse Kids.gov

http://www.whitehouse.gov/kids/

Whitehousekids.gov provides an educational opportunity for students to explore the White House and learn about the President. There are exciting activities for students and guides for teachers to help their students.

Kid's Click—American History

http://www.kidsclick.org/midamer.html

Kid's Click is a Web search made for kids by librarians. It is a great site to bookmark and use on a regular basis for homework help and general information searches. Some of its American History categories include Pilgrims, Colonial Period, the Revolutionary War, George Washington, Lewis and Clark, Westward Expansion, Oregon Trail, Gold Rush, Slavery, Abraham Lincoln, Civil War, Cowboys and Cowgirls, Labor Movement, Immigration, World War I, The Depression, World War II, the Holocaust, the Vietnam War, and Witch Trials.

Social Studies [cont.]

American History and Geography [cont.]

POTUS: Presidents of the United States

http://www.ipl.org/div/potus/

This resource has background information, election results, cabinet members, notable events, and interesting personal information on each of the presidents. Links to biographies, historical documents, audio and video files, and other presidential sites are also included.

National Park Service—Interpretation and Education

http://www.nps.gov/learn/home.htm

This site offers curriculum, fun and games, a guide to the National Parks Junior Ranger programs and other fun and educational media created by the National Park Service.

National Park Service—Web Ranger

http://65.39.199.136/webrangers/

Students will become Web Rangers and earn their Web Ranger Certificate by solving mysteries and puzzles, playing games, taking part in stories, and gathering secret words at this National Park site.

Net States

http://www.netstate.com/states/index.html

There is plenty of basic information on each state, including the state flag, symbol, and state history. It provides state statistics and other rankings. Their resources are perfect for students to use for a state comparison project. Challenge your students to take a test about each state to see what they know.

The U.S. Fifty

http://www.theus50.com/

This site offers facts, games, and quizzes to help students learn about the 50 states of the United States. This site is also a good reference for students to use for state reports.

Social Studies

Social Studies [cont.]

Ancient Civilizations

BBC Ancient History for Kids

http://www.bbc.co.uk/history/forkids/

This is a site for kids that can help them understand the basic concepts of each civilization that had an influence on British history. It includes facts and activities that are engaging and easy to understand.

Cyber Sleuths—Ancient Civilizations

http://cybersleuth-kids.com/sleuth/History/Ancient_Civilizations/index.htm

This site provides links to themes covering 13 ancient civilizations and groups of people. Students can select a specific civilization to explore, or they can choose several to compare and contrast. This site also has an Ancient Civilizations clip art link that your students can use, at **http://classroomclipart.com/cgi-bin/kids/imageFolio.cgi?direct=History/Ancient_Civilizations**.

British Museum

http://www.thebritishmuseum.ac.uk/world/world.html

The British Museum covers the history of Africa, the Americas, Asia, Britain, Egypt, Europe, Greece, Japan, the Near East, Pacific, and Rome. The collections and exhibits are fascinating and beautiful. Students will enjoy the interactive options that are available.

BBC Ancient History

http://www.bbc.co.uk/history/ancient/

This site has an easy-to-understand, extremely rich presentation for each of the following civilizations: Egyptian, Greek, British Prehistory, Roman, Viking, and Anglo-Saxon.

Ancient Civilizations Theme page

http://www.cln.org/themes/ancient.html

This theme page has links to two types of resources related to the study of ancient civilizations—curricular resources and lesson plans. This is a content–rich site.

Social Studies [cont.]

Famous People in History

Bio 4 Kids

http://www.biography.com/bio4kids/index.jsp

This site from the Biography Channel includes historical figures and contemporary icons. The resources here are informative and fun and should inspire students to learn more about these important people.

America's Story from America's Library—Meet Amazing Americans

http://www.americaslibrary.gov/cgi-bin/page.cgi/aa

At this site, students can discover inventors, politicians, performers, activists, and other everyday people who made America what it is today.

Geography—The World Around Us

Discovery School—Geography Lesson Plans

http://school.discovery.com/lessonplans/geog.html

This site has an excellent selection of lesson plans. Divided into three grade groupings, Discovery School includes objectives, materials, procedures, adaptations, evaluations, links, and more.

National Geographic Geography Lessons and Activities

http://www.nationalgeographic.com/resources/ngo/education/ideas.html

National Geographic's Geography Education Program helps educators create great resources, units, lessons, and activities so they can bring the sights and sounds of good geography into their classroom. The resources are grouped into three age spans. They also have additional resources for their website stories on Contact in the Amazon, Discovering Mexico, Gaza, Okavango, Tarantulas, the White House, and Wildlife Refuges.

Social Studies [cont.]

Geography—The World Around Us [cont.]

Education World—Geography Center

http://www.education-world.com/soc_sci/geography/index.shtml

Geography Center provides lesson plans, activities and projects, map resources, and teaching resources about other places to help you plan interesting, interactive geography lessons.

⚹ Yahoo! Kids—Around the World

http://kids.yahoo.com/directory/Around-the-World

Yahooligans is now Yahoo! Kids. The Around the World directory category at Yahoo! Kids produces hundreds of safe, kid-friendly history and geography sites. It is a great place for students to go when they are beginning a research project. This is also a good site to use for a scavenger hunt. You could make a list of facts for the scavenger hunt or have your students find facts to make the questions for a student-generated scavenger hunt. Creating the hunt questions is a higher-level thinking activity.

CIA World Factbook

https://www.cia.gov/cia/publications/factbook/index.html

Every student needs to gather information at the CIA World Factbook. It is always current, and it covers every region and country in the world. The same set of statistics is provided for each country. This is perfect data for students to use to do a comparative analysis of several countries.

CIA Home Page for Kids

https://www.cia.gov/kids-page/index.html

Young people often have a fascination with the CIA. This site provides students with information about the organization. There is a section for grades K–5 and 6–12. There is also a games section and a teacher-parent section too.

⚹ United Nations Cyber School Bus

http://cyberschoolbus.un.org/

This is the United Nations site for students and schools. It provides curriculum for themes like peace education, poverty, human rights, cities of the world, world hunger, indigenous people, discrimination, and model UN. Be sure you check out this site and involve your students in its activities and student groups.

Geography—The World Around Us (cont.)

Peace Corps—Kids World

http://www.peacecorps.gov/kids/

Children can send e-postcards, read folktales, download coloring pages, and test their geography skills with interactive games. Their sections include What is the Peace Corps? Make a Difference; Explore the World; Foods, Friends, and Fun; and Tell Me a Story. Try their Pack Your Bags game with your class. They can go to Nepal, South Africa, or Ecuador.

MapQuest

http://www.mapquest.com/

MapQuest includes an interactive atlas, a guide with street maps from all over the world, and a TripQuest that offers driving directions for the United States, Canada, and Mexico. Share the directions and trip-planning tools with your students. Encourage them to use these tools with their families.

History

Discovery School History Lessons

Ancient History

http://school.discovery.com/lessonplans/ancienthis.html

World History

http://school.discovery.com/lessonplans/worldhis.html

U.S. History

http://school.discovery.com/lessonplans/ushis.html

Discovery School has an excellent selection and variety of lesson plans at these three history sites. The lesson plans are divided into K–5, 6–8 and 9–12 groupings.

Education World—History

http://www.education-world.com/history/

This is a rich resource with superb world history lesson plans for teachers.

Social Studies [cont.]

History [cont.]

Library of Congress—The Learning Page

http://lcweb2.loc.gov/ammem/ndlpedu/

The Library of Congress Learning Page provides teachers with more than 7 million historical documents, photographs, maps, films, and audio recordings. There are lesson plans, activities, tools, ideas, and features that are useful for teaching American history.

PBS Teacher Source

http://www.pbs.org/teachers/socialstudies/

This is a multimedia resource for K–12 educators. PBS Teacher Source offers lessons and activities that are arranged by topic and grade level. Categories include American history, world history, history on television, and biographies.

Museums

Virtual Museum of Canada—Teachers' Center

http://www.virtualmuseum.ca/English/Teacher/index_flash.html

Several Canadian museums worked together to create this site. They have virtual exhibits, an image gallery, and a community memories section. Students can create their own museum, pick a theme, add descriptions, and choose their own layout. This is a great thinking activity for your students.

Smithsonian's National Museum of American History

http://americanhistory.si.edu/

At this site, you can use the museum's collections and research in your classroom. They offer teacher manuals and online activities. Your students can explore American history by following a time line of stories from the museum's exhibits, collections, and programs.

Smithsonian's Kid's Museum

http://americanhistory.si.edu/kids/index.cfm

Many of the museum's exhibitions have special activities. There is a History Explorer section, an Our Story in History section, and an Invention at Play section. These sections have great interactive activities for your students. Their Kids: Things to Do at Home section has fun interactive exhibits that can be explored on home computers.

Social Studies [cont.]

Museums [cont.]

Museum of London: Learning Online

http://www.museumoflondon.org.uk/learning/

The Museum of London tells the story of London from pre-historic times to the present day. This site has great materials for teachers and great activities for students.

The State Hermitage Museum—St. Petersburg Russia

http://hermitagemuseum.org/html_En/index.html

The State Hermitage Museum's Virtual Academy introduces students to the art and culture of ancient Rome, Russian emperors and Russian history during the 18th and 19th centuries, the times of knights, castles, and the crusades; and the geography, history, religion, and architecture of ancient Egypt. Students can create art with an interactive project on the site too.

Pioneer Life

Pioneer Life in Upper Canada

http://www.projects.yrdsb.edu.on.ca/pioneer/home_eng.htm

Students can investigate questions about Canadian aboriginals and pioneers. There is a curriculum guide for this third-grade history lesson. The site is interactive and well done.

Illinois State Museum—At Home in the Heartland

http://www.museum.state.il.us/exhibits/athome/index.html

This interactive exhibit is about family life in Illinois from the 1700s to the present. Students can meet people of the period, share in their decision making, and explore and compare their lifestyles with other areas in the country.

Camp Silos Activities

http://www.campsilos.org/search.htm

Many interactive activities for students are offered here to help them explore prairie life and pioneer farming. Materials relating to present-day farm life are also available for comparison.

Social Studies [cont.]

Pioneer Life [cont.]

Camp Silos Excursions

http://www.campsilos.org/excursions/index.htm

At this Camp Silos site, students can become the museum's curator who needs to sort through primary sources to create museum exhibits on pioneer life. Students can choose from three different interactive adventures.

The Environment

U.S. Environmental Protection Agency

http://www.epa.gov/

The U.S. Environmental Protection Agency provides up-to-date information about our environment. Students can use the Quick Finder to learn about topics and resources that are of interest to the agency. The following audience-specific links from the agency provide excellent resources for the classroom, with suggestions for getting students involved in community environmental service projects.

Fish and Wildlife Service—Education

http://www.fws.gov/educators/students.html

This site is for students of all ages. Students can explore and learn about fish, wildlife, plants, and their habitats, and how they can help conserve, protect, and enhance them.

Environment Canada—A Website for Youth

http://www.ec.gc.ca/youth/index_e.cfm

Students in Canada can participate with environmental youth organizations in their communities. They can expand their knowledge about the environment, get involved with the Youth Round Table on the Environment, and check out jobs and internships.

Social Studies [cont.]

(The Environment [cont.])

National Geographic Society

http://www.nationalgeographic.com/

Just scrolling through the main page of the National Geographic site is exciting. There are so many things to see and do. Students will love the quality of the stories covered at National Geographic, and they will enjoy the games and activities that are offered.

National Geographic Society for Kids

http://www.nationalgeographic.com/kids/

This site is truly amazing. National Geographic for Kids offers a wealth of information and engaging activities. There are great reading/comprehension learning opportunities here too. Be sure to check out all the links at this site—you and your students will love them all.

National Wildlife Federation

http://www.nwf.org/

This site offers tips on getting involved with enjoying and protecting our wildlife and the natural outdoors. Have your students explore what The National Wildlife Federation organization does and the impact it has had on the protection of wildlife.

National Wildlife Federation for Kids

http://www.nwf.org/kids/

The activities at this site for kids help them get involved with wildlife conservation. They can play games that help them understand what is happening to some of our wildlife and their habitats. There are also links to their children's magazines.

The Wildlife Conservation Society

http://www.wcs.org/

The Wildlife Conservation Society saves wildlife and wild lands through careful science, international conservation, education, and the management of the world's largest system of urban wildlife parks. This site offers a perspective on how everyone can help save wildlife. It is interesting for students to see who is saving wildlife in different parts of the world.

Social Studies [cont.]

The Environment [cont.]

The Wildlife Conservation Society—Kids Go Wild

http://www.kidsgowild.com/

Kids can get involved in saving wildlife and wild lands. They can find out what kids like them are doing to protect endangered animals; they can see and learn about cool animals; they can test their skills and creativity by playing online games, and they can read how the Wildlife Conservation Society does its part to save wildlife and wild lands.

World Wildlife Foundation

http://www.panda.org/news_facts/education/index.cfm

The World Wildlife Foundation is a global environmental conservation organization. It can be recognized by its panda logo. Teachers can find out about conservation and its role in our lives. Topics include endangered species and tackling environmental issues. Teachers choose their educational level to get resources, homework ideas, projects, and activities.

World Wildlife Foundation—Kids

http://www.panda.org/news_facts/multimedia/fun_games/index.cfm

Students will love playing the games at this site and finding out more about conservation issues like endangered species, global warming, and pollution. This site offers an exciting way to introduce wildlife conservation concepts. It is also a great starting point for younger students.

Sierra Club

http://www.sierraclub.org/

The Sierra Club has more than 750,000 members who are inspired by nature and who work together to protect our communities and the planet. The Sierra Club is America's oldest, largest, and most influential grassroots environmental organization. Use this site to help students understand how politics have helped protect and improve our environment.

Special Education

Introduction

The area of special education is so large and encompassing that it is almost impossible to reference it all. In this section of the book, sites have been organized into categories according to a specific impairment or disorder. Many students with special needs are now mainstreamed into the regular classroom. It is important that administrators, teachers, and parents have access to information that will best assist their special learners in having the most effective education process possible. Everyone needs to know what their role should be to help individuals in need of differentiated education. These sites will provide excellent resources for everyone.

Any educator involved with a student with special needs has probably been involved with the IEP process. The following IEP-related sites offer guidelines for writing and using IEPs and may provide additional ideas and a structure for writing or contributing to a plan.

SUGGESTED activity

These two sites offer great resources for the classroom teacher. Explore them both as a way to learn more about the visually impaired, and find programs and resources that are available to the blind, parents, and educators. The sites are as follows:
American Foundation for the Blind at **http://www.afb.org/**
Braille Bug at **http://www.afb.org/brailllebug/**
Share the activities at Braille Bug with your students. Have them write about their feelings about blindness and visual impairments. Poems or songs are great writing choices for this type of activity.

Special Education [cont.]

Assistive Technology

The Department of Education—Assistive Technology

http://www.ed.gov/policy/gen/guid/assistivetech.html

The Department of Education has made a commitment to support its obligation under Sections 504 and 508 of the Rehabilitation Act of 1973, as amended, to ensure the accessibility of its programs and activities to individuals with disabilities, specifically its obligation to acquire accessible electronic and information technology.

The Assistive Technology Program has grown to include a diversified set of services for staff, supervisors, and customers. Today, the program is considered a model and is emulated by many other federal agencies. This site provides visitors with very specific information about the Rehabilitation Act, with sections for students, parents, teachers, and administrators.

Alliance for Technology Access

http://www.ataccess.org

The Alliance for Technology Access (ATA) is the national network of community-based resource centers, developers, vendors, and associates dedicated to providing information and support services to children and adults with disabilities and increasing their use of standard, assistive, and information technologies.

Center for Applied Special Technology—CAST

http://www.cast.org/

Founded in 1984 as the Center for Applied Special Technology, CAST has earned international recognition for its development of innovative, technology-based educational resources and strategies based on the principles of Universal Design for Learning (UDL). Their mission is to expand learning opportunities for all individuals, especially those with disabilities, through the research and development of innovative, technology-based educational resources and strategies. CAST offers high-quality professional development and other resources to individuals, school districts, and postsecondary institutions to help educators at all grade levels meet the challenge of teaching diverse learners with Universal Design for Learning. Visit this site for more information.

Special Education [cont.]

Attention Deficit Disorder (ADD) and Attention Deficit Hyperactive Disorder AD/HD

ADD in School.com

http://www.addinschool.com/

ADD in School.com provides teachers with hundreds of classroom interventions to help their students with Attention Deficit Disorder. They have classroom interventions for elementary school children ages 5 to 12, and classroom interventions for junior high and high school students (teenagers ages 12 to 18).

New Ideas—Attention Deficit Hyperactivity Disorder Information Library

http://www.newideas.net/

This is an excellent site. It offers great information on Attention Deficit Hyperactivity Disorder organized into 10 easy lessons. They suggest that you take the time to go through all 10 of the lessons. Once you do, they feel you will know a lot about ADD and AD/HD, and have strategies to deal with it.

Children and Adults with Attention-Deficit/Hyperactivity Disorder—CHADD

http://www.chadd.org

Children and Adults with Attention-Deficit/Hyperactivity Disorder is the nation's leading nonprofit organization serving individuals with AD/HD and their families. CHADD has over 16,000 members in 200 local chapters throughout the United States. Chapters offer support for individuals, parents, teachers, professionals, and others. CHADD is a membership organization that produces the bimonthly magazine, *Attention,* for members, and sponsors an annual conference. The National Resource Center on AD/HD is the CDC-funded national clearinghouse for evidence-based information about AD/HD. This organization has a great section called Understand AD/HD, which includes the following subsections: Understanding AD/HD, ADD or AD/HD? Myths and Misunderstandings, Co-occurring Conditions and Genetics, AD/HD and School, Terms to Know, FAQs, and Research Studies. This is a good, comprehensive site to visit when you are beginning to learn about ADD and AD/HD.

Special Education [cont.]

Autism and Asperger's Disorder

Autism Society of America—The Voice of Autism

http://www.autism-society.org

This site is devoted to increasing public awareness of the day-to-day issues faced by individuals with autism, their families, and the professionals with whom they interact. The society provides excellent information about autism, as well as information about getting involved with the programs and activities they sponsor.

Center for the Study of Autism

http://www.autism.org

The Center for the Study of Autism (CSA) provides information about autism to parents and professionals, and conducts research on the efficacy of various therapeutic interventions. Much of their research is in collaboration with the Autism Research Institute in San Diego, California.

Their listings of resources and links are divided into the following categories: Subgroups and Related Disorders, Issues, Interventions, Temple Grandin, Sibling Center, Exclusive Interviews, and Other Links. This is a valuable site to visit.

Autism Education Network

http://www.autismeducation.net

The Autism Education Network's mission is to improve public special education programs and to influence public policy that affects individuals with autism. They use new technology and the Internet to connect people in order to affect change. The Autism Education Network is a parent-support organization that provides information and training about the best practices in autism treatment. They host an annual education conference every April, and they provide access to a community-based distance learning center, a message-board, and a communication service for families affected by autism-spectrum disorders.

Autism Today

http://www.autismtoday.com/

Autism Today is the leading source of objective information about Autism Spectrum Disorders, including Autistic Disorder, Asperger's Syndrome, Rett's Syndrome, Childhood Disintegrative Disorder, and other pervasive developmental disorders. This organization's website is designed to support, not replace the relationship between patient and physician. They offer a comprehensive online directory of programs, services, easy to locate professionals, schools, camps, recreational programs, and much more. They also have the following sections: Article Library, Ask the Experts, Online Gallery, Poems and Stories, and Web Logs. Check their site to keep up-to-date on conference offerings and other important events.

Special Education (cont.)

Down Syndrome

National Down Syndrome Society

http://www.ndss.org/

The mission of the National Down Syndrome Society is to help people with Down syndrome and their families through national leadership in education, research, and advocacy. The site offers information and resources on health, publications, development, and education and schooling.

Down Syndrome: Health Issues

http://www.ds-health.com/

This website was created and is maintained by Dr. Leshin, a pediatrician and father of a child with Down syndrome. His mission is to promote the health of children with Down syndrome and to empower parents of children with the condition with knowledge about it. Dr. Leshin' provides essays he and others knowledgeable about Down syndrome have written, reviews of scientific research about Down syndrome, Down syndrome health guidelines, controversies in Down syndrome, and other information such as related Internet sites and books.

Dyslexia

Dyslexia Teacher

http://www.dyslexia-teacher.com/

This site offers information and resources for helping dyslexic students, their parents, and their teachers. Teachers who want to know more about dyslexia should start exploring here.

Dyslexia Center

http://www.dyslexiacenter.org/main.shtml

The Dyslexia Awareness and Resource Center is geared to help students and adults with dyslexia and ADD, as well as their parents, teachers, and the professionals who work with them. They offer recent articles, newsletters, and resources that provide ideas that can be used directly in the classroom and ways a classroom teacher can seek additional help.

Special Education [cont.]

Dyslexia [cont.]

Reading from Scratch

http://www.dyslexia.org/index.shtml

Reading from Scratch (RfS/EL) is a program of science-based teaching techniques that can help make grade-level or higher reading possible. While this is a specific program, educators may find its approach interesting.

General Sites

U.S. Department of Education—Office of Special Education Programs

http://www.ed.gov/about/offices/list/osers/osep/index.html

This site is an excellent resource to check for possible funding opportunities. U.S. Department of Education—Office of Special Education Programs is "dedicated to improving results for infants, toddlers, children, and youth with disabilities ages birth through 21 by providing leadership and financial support to assist states and local districts. The Individuals with Disabilities Education Act (IDEA) authorizes formula grants to states and discretionary grants to institutions of higher education and other nonprofit organizations to support research, demonstrations, technical assistance and dissemination, technology and personnel development, and parent-training and information centers."

Office of Special Education Programs—Regional Resource and Federal Centers Network

http://www.rrfcnetwork.org/

Six regional resource centers and the federal resource center are funded by the Federal Office of Special Education Programs. Their purpose is to assist state education agencies in the improvement of education programs, practices, and policies that affect children and youth with disabilities. These centers offer consultation, information services, technical assistance, training, and product development.

General Sites (cont.)

Internet Special Education Resources (ISER)

http://www.iser.com/

Internet Special Education Resources is a nationwide directory of professionals, organizations, and schools that serve the learning disabilities and special education communities. They help parents and caregivers find local special education professionals to help with learning disabilities and attention deficit disorder assessment, therapy, advocacy, critical teen issues, and other special needs. They also offer a directory of professional resources, special needs software and assistive technology, and travel assistance for disabled persons.

Internet Resources for Special Children—IRSC

http://www.irsc.org/

The Internet Resources for Special Children website is dedicated to children with disabilities and other health-related disorders. Their mission is to improve the lives of these children by providing valuable information to parents, family members, caregivers, friends, educators, and medical professionals who provide them with services and support. The IRSC acts as a starting point that integrates information, resources, and communication opportunities to create positive changes and enhance public awareness and knowledge of children with disabilities and other health-related disorders. Their Online Communities is a place where questions can be asked and people can connect with other people who may have the same questions, thoughts, and experiences.

Family Village—A Global Community of Families with Disabilities

http://www.familyvillage.wisc.edu/

Family Village integrates information, resources, and communication opportunities on the Internet for persons with cognitive and other disabilities and their families, and for those that provide services and support. They include informational resources on specific diagnoses, communication connections, adaptive products and technology, adaptive recreational activities, education, worship, health issues, disability-related media and literature, and much more!

Special Education [cont.]

General Sites [cont.]

About Special Education

http://specialed.about.com/

This is a good site with special education resources, inclusion strategies, and classroom and parental support. Some of their topics include assistive technology, assessment, handling behavior, classroom management, disabilities, reading and literacy, giftedness, IEP IDEA, integration and inclusion, teacher strategies, worksheets, organizations, and special education acronyms. About Special Education offers some basic resources like goal-setting worksheets, checklists for LD, FAQs for parents and teachers, and behavior contracts.

Special Education in the Yahoo! Directory

http://dir.yahoo.com/Education/Special_Education/

Explore sites devoted to special education issues such as inclusion, assistive technology, learning disabilities, and individuals with disabilities at this Yahoo! directory listing.

Google Directory—Reference > Education > Special Education

www.google.com/Top/Reference/Education/Special_Education/

Google has a well-organized directory for special education. It is worth looking at to see if any sites or topics are included here that you have not have not seen anywhere else. If you have a specific question, use a keyword search at this site to find your answer.

Parentpals.com—Special Education Guide

http://parentpals.com/gossamer/pages/

This special education website focuses on parent and professional support for special needs children. Ameri-Corp Speech and Hearing sponsors this site. This site's resource section has a choice of more than 1,126 articles and links. It also has sections for continuing education, special education products, a bookstore, teaching games, tips, a message board, and a comprehensive dictionary. The dictionary is a great resource for anyone not familiar with special education terminology.

Special Education [cont.]

General Sites [cont.]

The Disability Resources Monthly—Guide to Disability Resources on the Internet

http://www.disabilityresources.org/

Disability Resources Monthly is a nonprofit organization that monitors, reviews, and reports on resources available to people with disabilities. They distribute information about these resources to libraries, disability organizations, health and social service professionals, consumers, and family members. This site includes a searchable database of resources, weekly features, news updates, a regional resource directory, and information on publications.

disABILITY Information and Resources

http://www.makoa.org/index.html

This site offers a long list of articles about disabilities and links to disability resources on the Web that include databases, resource sites, events, products, and services. Special pages are also included with links to information on accessible Web page design. These pages were created and are maintained solely by Jim Lubin, who is a C2 quadriplegic, completely paralyzed from the neck down and dependent on a ventilator to breathe. He uses a keyboard/mouse emulator with a sip-and-puff switch to type Morse codes. This site has been online since 1994, and the information is updated frequently.

Special Education Network

http://www.specialednet.com/Resources.htm

The Special Education Network is a website dedicated to providing information and resources on the education of children with special needs. Its sections include Inclusive Education, Parent Education and Support, Advocacy Organizations, Disability Information and Referral, Community Living, Government Agencies, and Related Links.

Gifted and Talented

National Association for the Gifted

http://www.nagc.org/

The National Association for the Gifted is a membership organization. It has resources for administrators, educators, and parents, and is involved with providing conventions and seminars. It also has an advocacy and legislation group and provides information on gifted programs by state.

Special Education [cont.]

Gifted and Talented [cont.]

National Research Center for the Gifted and Talented—Educational Resource Links

http://www.gifted.uconn.edu/nrcgt/edsites.html

This site is part of the National Research Center for the Gifted and Talented. It provides links for parents, students, and researchers interested in gifted education.

Health Problems

Kids Health.org

http://www.kidshealth.org/

KidsHealth is the largest and most-visited site on the Web that provides doctor-approved health information about children from before birth through adolescence. Created by The Nemours Foundation's Center for Children's Health Media, KidsHealth provides families with accurate, up-to-date, and jargon-free health information they can use. KidsHealth has been on the Web since 1995 and has been accessed by about 300,000,000 visitors. Use this site to update your information about health issues that might present themselves in your classroom.

Kids Health Problems

http://www.kidshealth.org/kid/health_problems/

In special education, educators deal with students with a variety of health problems both serious and not. This site provides basic information for educators and parents about health problems related to the following categories: Allergies and Immune System, Asthma, Birth Defects and Genetic Problems, Bladder, Kidneys and Urinary Tract, Blood, Bones, Muscles, and Joints, Brain and Nervous System, Cancer, Diabetes, Glands and Hormones, Heart and Lungs, Infections, Learning and Emotional Problems, Sight, Speech and Hearing, Skin, Stomach, Intestines and Liver, and Teeth and Mouth. All educators should familiarize themselves with the information that is available at this site.

ASL American Sign Language

http://www.lifeprint.com/

This site provides information about sign language, has free lesson plans, an ASL dictionary, and resources as well as information on deaf culture, history, grammar, and terminology. It is a great resource for the classroom teacher or a parent wanting to introduce sign language to his or her children.

Special Education [cont.]

Hearing Impairment

National Association of the Deaf

http://www.nad.org/

National Association of the Deaf is a national membership organization. It focuses on advocacy, American Sign Language, Interpreting, Captioning, Mental Health, Community and Culture, Education, and Technology.

IEP—Individualized Education Program

IEP Online Training

http://www.calstat.org/iep/

California Services for Technical Assistance and Training provides this six-lesson online training program. Its self-paced Web module will assist the learner in understanding the Individuals with Disabilities Education Act (IDEA), and the components of a performance goal and how this format applies to the mandates of the IDEA. This Web module is designed to take approximately four to six hours to complete. Its goals and objectives are family friendly, and easy to follow and use.

Cal State IEP Resources

http://www.calstat.org/iep/resources.html

This site has both national and state resources related to Individualized Education Programs, resources related to IDEA 2004, and specific resources for California issues.

ED.GOV—A Parent's IEP Guide

http://www.ed.gov/parents/needs/speced/iepguide/index.html

This extensive guide explains the IEP process, a critical process that is needed to ensure effective teaching, learning, and better results for all children with disabilities. This guide is designed to help teachers, parents, and anyone involved in the education of a child with a disability develop and carry out an IEP. The information in this guide is based on what is required by our nation's special education law—the Individuals with Disabilities Education Act, or IDEA.

Family Village—Individual Education Plans

http://www.familyvillage.wisc.edu/education/iep.html

This site provides links to many of the best websites that deal with the topic of IEPs. It also provides links to software that can be used for writing IEPs.

Special Education (cont.)

IEP—Individualized Education Program (cont.)

1 edweb—Electronic IEP Forms

http://www.1edweb.com/

Districts and schools might find that 1edweb electronic forms may help educators by converting their paper-based IEP forms into electronic templates. Many forms are available for free. Check out their Functional Behavior Assessment Forms at **http://www.1edweb.com/fba%20forms.htm**. Other form packages are available for a reasonable price.

New Zealand Minister of Education IEP Guidelines

http://www.minedu.govt.nz/index.cfm?layout=documentanddocumentid=7359anddata=l

These guidelines are for schools, parents, and specialists who support students with special education needs. These guidelines are intended to assist with planning for all special education students, whatever their needs. This site is well organized and has great ideas. It can be of use to anyone involved in the IEP process.

Physical Impairment

Disability Info.gov

http://www.disabilityinfo.gov/

DisabilityInfo.gov is the federal government's one-stop website for people with disabilities and their families, employers, veterans, workforce professionals, and many others. To support the goals of the New Freedom Initiative, President George W. Bush directed federal agencies to create DisabilityInfo.gov in order to connect people with disabilities to the information and resources they need to actively participate in the workforce and in their communities.

American Association of People with Disabilities

http://www.aapd-dc.org/

This is the home page for the American Association of People with Disabilities. This organization has political influence and offers many resources to its members. More than 100,000 members belong to this organization.

Special Education [cont.]

Physical Impairment [cont.]

United Cerebral Palsy—UCP

http://www.ucp.org/

United Cerebral Palsy is the leading source of information on cerebral palsy and is a pivotal advocate for the rights of persons with any disability. As one of the largest health charities in America, the UCP's mission is to advance the independence, productivity, and full citizenship of people with disabilities. This site offers great resources related to education, health and wellness, parenting and families, products and services, sports and leisure, transportation, and travel.

National Organization on Disability—NOD

http://www.nod.org/

National Organization on Disability—NOD focuses on community development, economic participation, and access to independence. Education is the key to independence and future success; it is critical to obtaining work, and affects how much money one can earn. Before the passage of the Individuals with Disabilities Education Act (IDEA) in 1975, which granted all children with disabilities a free, appropriate public education, many children with disabilities did not attend school because the buildings or class activities were inaccessible. Even now, 22 percent of Americans with disabilities fail to graduate high school, compared to 9 percent of those without disabilities. The National Organization on Disability believes that with enforced legislation, accessible classrooms, the respect of educators, and advances in assistive technology, students with disabilities can close that gap. They offer resources and information to assist in that effort. This site provides a good reference point for anyone involved in education of the disabled. It is a good place to read about what is expected, why we have to work so hard in providing a functional and safe environment, and why it is fair to do so.

Visual Impairments and Blindness

American Foundation for the Blind—AFB

http://www.afb.org/

The American Foundation for the Blind (AFB) is a national nonprofit organization that expands possibilities for people with vision loss. AFB's priorities include broadening access to technology; improving the quality of information and tools for the professionals who serve people with vision loss; and promoting independent and healthy living for people with vision loss by providing them and their families with relevant and timely resources.

Online Reference Sites for Teachers and Students

Introduction

The Internet has changed our lives. We now have the ability to connect with the world and learn about anything. However, we do not always have the tools or the skills to find what we need. Everyone needs easy access to sites that will provide them with resources that they need the most.

This section includes the following educational resources: encyclopedias, dictionaries and word-related sites, online grammar, punctuation, and spelling help, writing format and style guides, internet libraries, news sites, newspapers and magazines for adults and kids, authors' references, biographies, government-related reference sites, image resources, and music resources.

There are many phenomenal sites here. Take your time exploring them. You may be surprised at what can be useful for your students and for you.

SUGGESTED activity

Create a list of websites that would help make your day easier. Start with a variety of sites, work with them, and then narrow your list to the ones you used the most. Finish by adding these sites to your bookmarks or favorites list. You can also create a document with the names of the sites and their links. Creating a document creates a way to share sites with others. At the same time, you can create a list of important resource sites for your students. For example, if you are an English teacher, you might include a dictionary site, a writing process site, a grammar site, and a reference-citation site on your student website list.

Students love to explore online magazines. A great enrichment or homework activity is to have students review the magazine sites and select their favorites. You can do many activities with your students. Your students can write a review, an advertisement, or a commercial to draw attention to their selected favorite, graph their individual/class choices, or create a "What I learned at my magazine site" poster or website. The possibilities are limitless. Magazine sites are a great way for students to become more aware of the world around them.

Online Reference Sites for Teachers and Students [cont.]

General Reference

Education Index—Education Resources by Subject

http://www.educationindex.com/education_resources.html

Education Resources by Subject is a topic-by-topic breakdown of the best educational sites on the Web. Those at this site continually review new sites and add resources. They also appreciate and use visitors' comments and link suggestions.

Answers.Com—Teachers Tool Kit

http://www.teachers.answers.com/

Teachers all over the world use Answers.Com—Teachers Tool Kit to find facts, explanations, and definitions on more than 4 million topics. The site was given the 2006 Codie Award for Best Education Reference or Search Service. There is a great range of resources at this site. Answers.Com offers free classroom worksheets like Active Reading and Research Right worksheets, designed to help students build research and reading comprehension skills. They also offer tools for teachers. You can access their classroom website/blog, online presentations, and correspondence on your computer.

BJ Pinchbeck's Homework Help

http://school.discovery.com/homeworkhelp/bjpinchbeck/

BJ Pinchbeck started this site with his dad several years ago. Now it is on The Discovery Channel School site. It is for anyone who needs help with homework. "If you can't find it here, then you just can't find it" is the promise on the site's header. The homework links at this site include art/music, computer science and the Internet, English, foreign languages, health and P.E., math, news, recess, reference, science, search engines, and social studies. This is a great site for your students to bookmark or add to their favorites list.

Reference Desk

http://www.refdesk.com/facts.html

Virtual Facts Online has encyclopedias, atlases, biographies and much more. It is part of refdesk.com, which is a source of many other reference materials. Besides being an index with many different topic areas, it also has Essential Reference Tools, Fast Facts, and Reference Desk sections.

Online Reference Sites for Teachers and Students (cont.)

Authors' References and Biographies

Children's Literature Web Guide—Authors and Illustrators on the Web

http://www.acs.ucalgary.ca/~dkbrown/authors.html

The Internet has become a great source of information about a great many children's writers and illustrators. The websites listed at this site include authors' personal websites and websites maintained by fans, scholars, and readers. This is a great site for anyone interested in finding out more about a particular author. You will find information about the authors that your students are studying, lesson plans related to the author or the author's books, and engaging activities for students.

Library Spot—Caldecott Medal Winners

http://www.libraryspot.com/lists/caldecott.htm

The Caldecott Medal honors the best children's picture book of the year. The Association for Library Service to Children, a division of the American Library Association, awards the medal annually. This site provides a list of winners from 1938 to the present as well as education/library related articles, questions, and lists.

Library Spot—Newbery Medal Winners

http://www.libraryspot.com/lists/newbery.htm

The Newbery Medal honors the author making the most distinguished contribution to American literature for children. It too is an annual award made by the Association for Library Service to Children, a division of the American Library Association.

Library Spot—Biographies

http://www.libraryspot.com/biographies/

LibrarySpot.com is a virtual library resource center for educators and students, librarians, and families. It attempts to bring the best library and reference sites together under common topics in one user-friendly spot. Sites featured on LibrarySpot.com are hand-selected and reviewed by their editorial team for their exceptional quality, content, and utility. Students can search this biography section by general sites, by type of biography, and by ethnicity.

Authors' References and Biographies (cont.)

Biography.com

http://www.biography.com/

This site focuses on people in the news today and in the past. Students can browse by using the alphabetical index or by category. They can see videos or explore topics such as actors/actresses, the Oscars, bio4kids, black history, U.S. Presidents, women's history, celebrity fact or fiction, and weekly highlights. They can also have fun with the games link, the TV section, and the Born on this Day section. This site is exciting and vibrant. All students, particularly middle school and high school students, will enjoy the activities available at this site.

Dictionaries and Word-Related Sites

Merriam-Webster Online

http://www.merriam-webster.com/

Besides the online versions of the *Merriam-Webster Dictionary*, *Thesaurus*, and *Spanish/English Dictionary*, the Merriam-Webster site is also linked to the *Unabridged Dictionary*, the *Learner's Dictionary*, *Word Central for Kids*, *Collegiate Dictionary*, and the *Encyclopedia Britannica*. This is a great resource for both teachers and students. Word of the Day, Word Games, Open Dictionary, Spelling Bee Hive, and Word for the Wise are a just a few of the interactive, motivating word-related activities that are available at the site.

Reference.Com

http://www.reference.com/

Reference.com has a dictionary, thesaurus, and an online Web directory. It features a Word of the Day, language fun and games, language translation dictionaries and instant translators, and crossword, legal, and medical dictionaries.

Wordsmyth

http://www.wordsmyth.net/

Wordsmyth offers a searchable dictionary and thesaurus where words can be looked up by using the exact or approximate spelling. They also have Wordsmith's Children's Dictionary and a word search tool that is geared to younger children. Both are easy to use. This site offers other education and study tools too—a Glossary Maker, a Vocabulary Quiz Maker, an Anagram Solver, and a Crossword Puzzle Helper.

Online References

Online Reference Sites for Teachers and Students [cont.]

Dictionaries and Word-Related Sites [cont.]

OneLook—Reverse Dictionary

http://www.onelook.com/reverse-dictionary.shtml

OneLook's reverse dictionary lets you describe a concept to get a list of words and phrases related to that concept. Description can be a few words, a sentence, a question, or even just a single word. All you need to do is to type in a description and hit the Find Words button. In most cases, you will get back a list of related terms with the best matches shown first. Students can have fun with this site and use it as a way to practice vocabulary.

Reference Desk Dictionary and Language Resources

http://www.refdesk.com/factdict.html

This site provides two dictionaries, a thesaurus, and an acronym finder. It also provides more than 180 links to grammar, styles, and other language-related sites.

Encyclopedias

Encarta

http://encarta.msn.com/

Encarta has everything, including an encyclopedia, a dictionary and thesaurus, a world atlas, multimedia, quizzes, top-10 lists, and an education section. This is a site all teachers and students should become familiar with as a basic starting point for researching materials and finding out about what is happening in the world. Encarta is for the mos part free but you can purchase a membership for more extensive resources.

Yahoo Education

http://education.yahoo.com/

Yahoo Education offers a great dictionary—*American Heritage Dictionary of the English Language*, an encyclopedia—*Columbia Encyclopedia*, a thesaurus—*Roget's II: The New Thesaurus*, a *World Fact Book*, a Spanish dictionary—*The American Heritage Spanish Dictionary: Spanish/English, Inglés/Español*, a quotations reference guide—*The Columbia World of Quotations*, an anatomy reference guide—*Gray's Anatomy*, and a conversion calculator. This site is a great all-inclusive site for finding information.

Online Reference Sites for Teachers and Students [cont.]

Encyclopedias [cont.]

Encyclopedia.com

http://www.encyclopedia.com/about.aspx

Encyclopedia.com provides users with more than 57,000 frequently updated articles from the Columbia Encyclopedia. Each article is enhanced with links to newspaper and magazine articles, as well as pictures and maps. The links to newspaper and magazine articles provide a useful perspective for classroom use.

Kid Info—School Subject

http://www.kidinfo.com/SchoolSubjects.html

A lot of precious time can be wasted searching and sifting through Web links to find appropriate information. Kid Info is a homework and research assistant that is different from other homework and research assistant sites because it is organized according to the specific curriculum covered in elementary, middle, and secondary schools. This is a good site to bookmark for student classroom and homework use.

Teacher TidBytes

http://www.teachertidbytes.com/

Teacher TidBytes is an excellent starting point for students, teachers, and parents who want to spend quality time on the Web. The site links users directly to pages that offer valuable curriculum-related topics and resources. The site provides Internet resources based upon classroom curriculum, kids pages, student-teacher tutorials, and Web-integrated lesson plans. Links found at Kid Info and Teacher TidBytes are checked weekly. Dead links are removed, and new sites are added on a weekly basis.

Information Please—Dictionary Encyclopedia and Almanac

http://www.infoplease.com/

Information Please puts together the Information Please Almanacs—sports, entertainment and general knowledge, with the *Random House Webster's College Dictionary* and the *Columbia Encyclopedia*. This is a great resource for classroom assignments. They claim they have "all the knowledge you need!"

Online References

Online Reference Sites for Teachers and Students (cont.)

Encyclopedias (cont.)

Britannica Encyclopedia

http://www.britannica.com

Britannica Encyclopedia was a popular encyclopedia for home use before computers and the Internet made them almost obsolete. This is an encyclopedia with a membership fee. However, it also offers a number of free sites for each topic searched.

Wikipedia

http://en.wikipedia.org/wiki/Main_Page

Wikipedia is very popular these days. It is the only encyclopedia that is not reviewed by experts but by thousands of volunteers. With rare exceptions, its articles can be edited by anyone with access to the Internet simply by clicking the "edit this page" link. This encyclopedia's articles can be added to, changed, and edited by individuals. The concept is part of the newest trend on the Internet—wikis and blogs. Wikipedia's information is as or sometimes more extensive that many encyclopedias. It covers a wide range of topics and often includes appropriate, usable photographs and graphics. This Wikipedia site is written in English. It started in 2001 and currently contains more than 1,752,464 articles. Wikipedias are available in other languages too.

The Awesome Library

http://www.awesomelibrary.org/

The Awesome Library organizes the Web with 31,000 carefully reviewed resources. It has a section for kids and teens, and some of its resource categories include the arts, English, math, science, social studies, geography, health and P.E., technology, languages, authors, reference, and news.

Government-Related Reference Sites

GovSpot

http://www.govspot.com/

GovSpot.com is a nonpartisan government information portal designed to simplify the search for the best and most relevant government information online. This free resource offers a great collection of top government and civic resources.

Government-Related Reference Sites [cont.]

CIA World Factbook

http://www.cia.gov/cia/publications/factbook/index.html

The CIA World Factbook has facts about countries in the world. This site is great for finding facts for a specific country report or information about more than one country for comparison.

First Government for Kids

http://www.kids.gov/

This is the U.S. Government's Kids' Portal. It provides links to Federal kids' sites, along with some of the best kids' sites from other organizations. Its websites are grouped into 20 different subject areas. Students should try the Web Treasure Hunt on this site.

Ben's Guide to U.S. Government

http://bensguide.gpo.gov/

This site provides learning tools and activities for students in grades K–2, 3–5, 6–8, and 9–12. There is also a teacher and parent section. Its resources teach how our government works and how to use of the primary source materials of the Government Printing Office. Ben's Guide provides a link to U.S. government websites developed for kids.

NASA

http://www.nasa.gov/home/index.html

NASA is a great reference for anything space related. It has sections for kids, students, and educators. It features such sections as Life on Earth, Humans in Space, Exploring the Universe, Missions, Latest News, and Multimedia. Best of all, for the space enthusiast, there is a My NASA section. Students can register for My NASA and get all the NASA information they want. As a member, students can customize a My NASA page with the NASA channels and content that interests them.

Online Reference Sites for Teachers and Students [cont.]

History and Geography

Museum Spot

http://www.museumspot.com/

MuseumSpot.com is a free information resource center that organizes the search for the best and most useful museum information on the Web. Museum Spot provides a guide to museums and other cultural information on the Web.

The History Channel

http://www.history.com/

This is a great resource for students. It has a search engine that is good for looking up specific reference material. It also has sections such as Military and War, Mysteries of History, U.S. History, Culture, World History, and Political and Historic Figures.

The Best History Web Sites

http://www.besthistorysites.net/

Best of History Web Sites is an award-winning portal that contains annotated links to over 1,000 history websites as well as links to hundreds of quality K–12 history lesson plans, teacher guides, history activities, history games, and history quizzes. The Best of History Web Sites was ranked number one by Google for history websites. This site is well worth a visit.

Kathy Schrock's Guide for Educators—American History

http://school.discovery.com/schrockguide/history/hista.html

Kathy Schrock organizes this collection of websites into American History, General History and Social Studies, and World and Ancient History. Like her other collections, this one is excellent.

Digital History—An Online American History Textbook

http://www.digitalhistory.uh.edu/

Digital History is an interactive, multimedia history of the United States from the Revolution to the present. It offers a variety of ways for students and teachers to study history. The site presents interactive timelines and guided readings as well as primary source materials, active learning opportunities, visual histories, and an incredible resource section. This is a great site for all American history teachers and students.

Online References

Online Reference Sites for Teachers and Students (cont.)

History and Geography (cont.)

America's Story from America's Library

http://www.americaslibrary.gov

America's Story from America's Library—the Library of Congress—provides students with stories from America's past by using their Meeting Amazing Americans, Jumping Back in Time, Exploring the States, Joining America at Play, and Seeing, Hearing, and Singing sections. This site was designed for young people, but there are great stories for people of all ages. The Library of Congress encourages children and their families to explore this site together. America's Story is fun, interesting, and interactive, and it should be shared with students and parents.

Map Quest

http://www.mapquest.com/

MapQuest is probably one of the more widely used Internet sites today. People use it to find directions and explore towns and cities worldwide. It displays addresses on a map, provides a view of nearby businesses, and gives driving directions and maps. Students should know about this site and be able to use it.

Google Earth

http://earth.google.com/

Google Earth needs to be downloaded from the Google site, but it is worth it because your students will love it. Google Earth combines satellite imagery, maps, and Google Search to display photos of specific geographic locations. Students can go from space to their own neighborhood by typing in an address and zooming in on the image provided. They can search for specific places such as schools, parks, restaurants, and hotels. They can also tilt and rotate the view from different perspectives. Students love to search and then save and share their searches and favorites with others in class.

Online Reference Sites for Teachers and Students *(cont.)*

History and Geography *(cont.)*

National Geographic Xpeditions Maps

http://www.nationalgeographic.com/xpeditions/atlas/

Students can search for black and white maps of specific areas. These maps are suitable for printing for use in the classroom and in student projects.

Image Resources

Google Images

http://images.google.com/

This is one of the best places for students to look for images. Make sure your students know the difference between image types like JPEG or GIF, and that they know to download the largest image size available. Large images are needed if they are going to be used in a slideshow or movie project. Make sure your students also save their image resource information so they can get back to their image if necessary. Encourage them to save the name of the image, its Web address, and the date that it was downloaded.

Yahoo—Image Search

http://images.search.yahoo.com/

Like Google, Yahoo also has an image search tool. If you cannot find what you are looking for at Google, try Yahoo's Image Search.

Pic Search

http://www.picsearch.com/

Pic Search is an image search engine that is family friendly, simple to use, and informative. This image search service searches more than 1.7 billion pictures.

Getty Images—Royalty Free Creative Images

http://creative.gettyimages.com/source/frontdoor/DefaultRfLanding.aspx

Using this site, you can search the royalty-free images, photos, and illustrations that are in the Getty collection.

Online References

Online Reference Sites for Teachers and Students (cont.)

Image Resources (cont.)

Pics4Learning

http://www.pics4learning.com/index.php

Pics4Learning is a copyright-friendly educational image library for teachers and students. The Pics4Learning collection consists of thousands of images that have been donated by students, teachers, and amateur photographers. The images are organized by category to make them easy to search.

Discovery School—Clip Art

http://school.discovery.com/clipart/

Students can choose from thousands of pieces of clip art and animations that are organized under 20 different categories. Students will find this clip-art site a great resource for adding interest to their documents or multimedia projects.

American Memory

http://memory.loc.gov/ammem/browse/

American Memory provides free access through the Internet to written and spoken words, sound recordings, still and moving images, prints, maps, and sheet music that have become digital records of American history and creativity. The materials come from the collections of the Library of Congress and other institutions. Students can browse the American Memory collection by topic, time period, place, or the type of collection.

Springfield Township Virtual Library

http://www.sdst.org/shs/library/cfimages.html

http://www.sdst.org/shs/library/clipart.html

The Springfield Township Virtual Library is amazing. Its resources for images and clip art have much to offer. Students and teachers can use so much from this site in projects and activities.

Online Reference Sites for Teachers and Students [cont.]

Image Resources [cont.]

Media Builder

http://www.mediabuilder.com/tile1.html

While this is a membership site, MediaBuilder has many free image files, backgrounds, animated gifs, lines, borders, icons, 3D clip art, and online tools. Users can enhance their email, Web pages, documents, and *PowerPoint* presentations with these images.

Classroom Clip Art

http://classroomclipart.com/

This great site has an education focus. Its only drawback is that it does charge a yearly fee for use. You might want to explore what it has to see if a membership would be worthwhile. They have no pop-ups or advertisements, and they advertise a fast search engine, hundreds of animated clip art, and thousands of photographs. They add hundreds of new images and graphics every month, and offer a personal light box to store images. You might want to check them out to see if a membership would be worth the cost.

Kid's Domain Clip Art Collection

http://www.kidsdomain.com/clip/

Kid's Domain is great for families. Besides its clip art section, they have many more resource and activity pages to visit.

Teacher Files—Clip Art

http://www.teacherfiles.com/clip_art.htm

This is one of the largest collection of free clip art on the Internet. A few of its sections include School and Education Clip Art, Subjects and Curriculum Areas, Animated Clip Art, Titles, Signs, Word Art, Word Art Generator, People Clip Art, Holiday and Seasons Clip Art, and Icons and Bullets. Use this site to jazz up your work and make it more interesting.

Online Reference Sites for Teachers and Students (cont.)

Internet Libraries

Internet Public Library Reference Center

http://www.ipl.org/div/subject/browse/ref00.00.00/

The Internet Public Library Reference Center includes basic research tools such as almanacs, dictionaries, and encyclopedias. It was founded at the University of Michigan's School of Information. It began as an educational initiative designed to provide students and professionals a place to explore and learn about the practice of librarianship in the digital age. Thousands of students have been involved in designing, building, creating and maintaining this site and its various services. In addition, hundreds of volunteer librarians throughout the world have been involved remotely; answering reference questions through the Ask a Question service. Be sure you bookmark this site and that your students are aware of its capabilities. This is one of the best reference sites for students to use.

Kid Space—Internet Public Library

http://www.ipl.org/div/kidspace/

This is an excellent site to bookmark for your students' use too. Kid Space has a number of worthwhile subject collections that are helpful for school projects—Reference, The World, Computer and the Internet, Health and Nutrition, Reading Zone, Math and Science, Art and Music, Sports and Recreation, and Fun Stuff. It also has special sections that are good for challenging students and giving them exciting activities online. Some of these sections include Science Fair, Stately Knowledge, Learning HTML, Orca Search, Poison Prevention, Author Page, Culture Quest, Story Hour, Say Hello around the World, and U.S. Presidents.

Library Spot

http://www.libraryspot.com/

Library Spot is a free virtual library resource center for educators, students and their families. It is considered one of the best library and reference resources on the web. It includes top-notch dictionaries, encyclopedias, newspapers, maps, quotations and much more.

Online Reference Sites for Teachers and Students (cont.)

Internet Libraries (cont.)

Math Forum Internet Library

http://Mathforum.org/library/

The Internet Math Library is a great resource for teachers, students, and parents who are looking for websites across the Internet on math topics. You can choose a math content topic, a math education topic, a resource type, or a grade level.

How Stuff Works

http://www.howstuffworks.com/

How Stuff Works is a great resource for the inquisitive mind. Students can find out how a telephone works, how the inside of your refrigerator stays cold, or other interesting things. This is an intriguing site that students should visit and explore.

Music Resources

Internet Public Library Music Resources

http://www.ipl.org

The Internet Public Library allows you to search for categories on the Internet of your interest. To get rich resources about music, click on Arts and Humanities—Fine Arts—Music. Or click Leisure—Entertainment and Leisure News—Music. You will find audio equipment and technology, genres, performance, musicians and composers, and collectors and collecting.

Educational Cyber Playground—Music Education Sites

http://www.edu-cyberpg.com/Music/m_sites.html

This site offers a wealth of music resources—free music downloads, classroom ideas and resources, starting a band, piano lessons, and world music, to mention a few. Check it out for answers to any of your music-related questions.

Online Reference Sites for Teachers and Students (cont.)

Music Resources (cont.)

Free Kids Music

http://freekidsmusic.com/

At this site, artists share songs with the intent of introducing you to their artistry. This provides a great opportunity for you to provide music to your students and their families.

The Children's Music Web

http://childrensmusic.org/

This site focuses on listing children's music websites that have links to many of the best music-for-kids resources online for teachers, parents, musicians, and kids.

Download.com

http://music.download.com/

This site has more than 75,000 free MP3 music downloads. It is divided by genre with more than 20 categories available. Once a genre is selected, visitors can view by artist or group and then select from the available free tracks. This site is easy to use.

News Sites

CNN News

http://www.cnn.com/

CNN.com is among the world's leaders in online news and information delivery. It delivers the latest breaking news and information on the latest stories. CNN News has 20 topic sections. Students can watch the latest news videos, or they can participate in Anderson Cooper's 360 Degrees Podcast, which provides high-speed highlights on world news. Use this site to help your students develop good news collecting habits. Knowing what is going on in the world is so important, and not all students have newspapers at home to find out about world news. This site offers a wonderful alternative.

Online Reference Sites for Teachers and Students [cont.]

News Sites [cont.]

Speak Out

http://www.pbs.org/newshour/extra/students/arts/index.html

Have your students try Speak Out. Student can contribute their work in four areas: Editorial Page—where students express opinions on important current events; My Story—where students share experiences that have influenced them personally; Debating the News—where students present different perspectives on an issue; and Poetry—where students can be creative with their words.

Stories

http://www.pbs.org/newshour/extra/index.html

Extra stories are short explanatory pieces that help students understand a current events issue happening right now and why it is important to their lives. Stories are archived by school topic.

NewzCrew

http://www.newzcrew.org

NewzCrew is an online chat group for and by young people. Participating students can join other teens from around the world in a guided online discussion about current events and learn how to get more involved in the democratic process.

Daily Buzz

http://www.pbs.org/newshour/extra/

The Daily Buzz is a brief news clip that presents something interesting for them to investigate and discuss. Found in the upper right corner of Extra Pages, the Daily Buzz stories change Monday through Friday.

Big Eye

http://bigeye.com/news.htm

Be sure to check out this site. It presents breaking news with the latest from the Associated Press Wires, AOL News, the Bloomberg Report, and the Headline Spot. It also provides up-to-date financial news and a section with news search engines.

Online References

Online Reference Sites for Teachers and Students (cont.)

News Sites (cont.)

TIME for Kids—News

http://www.timeforkids.com/TFK/news/index.html

TIME for Kids has great up-to-date national news. They also have a News section, Poll Zone, Kid Scoops, Specials, Games, and a Homework Helper section. This site also has sections for teachers with teaching resources, lesson plans, worksheets, and graphic organizers. For parents, there is a Go Places section where parents can take a virtual voyage around the world with their child.

Scholastic News

http://teacher.scholastic.com/scholasticnews/index.asp

This site includes News, Special Reports, Kids' Press Corps, and Games and Quizzes. Use this site to provide your students with an interactive connection to the news.

Science News—The Why Files

http://whyfiles.org/

This site has been on the web for 10 years. It provides students with the science behind the news. The stories are interesting and can help students understand the controversy behind such things as the ozone layer, the spinach *E. coli* scare, the electric car, skin cancer, hurricanes, and school violence. This site is a great spot for students to go when they want to look up relevant and interesting science information.

Ask an Expert

http://www.askanexpert.com/

Students often have questions that they cannot answer with research. Ask an Expert can be used to connect them to experts who will help to answer their questions. This site has links to hundreds of real-world experts ranging from astronauts to zookeepers who volunteer their time to answer questions. This kid-friendly site is also great for the student who is always asking those hard-to-answer questions.

Online References

Online Reference Sites for Teachers and Students (cont.)

Newspapers and Magazines

Yahoo—News and Media and Magazine Directory

http://dir.yahoo.com/News_and_Media/magazines/

Browse Yahoo's extensive directory of magazines. It covers a broad range of subjects including education, women, traveling, parenting, entertainment, fashion, and home and garden.

Internet Public Library: Newspapers

http://www.ipl.org/div/news/

The Internet Public Library features online newspapers from around the world. Users can search the site by country, location or paper name.

Internet Public Library: Magazines

http://www.ipl.org/div/serials/

The Internet Public Library features a searchable, subject-categorized directory of websites with links to magazines, journals, and e-zines.

Internet/Magazines—WebReference.com

http://www.webreference.com/internet/magazines/

This site features magazines that are computer- and Internet-related. It has a general section as well as one for PCs and one for Macs.

Online Reference Sites for Teachers and Students (cont.)

Newspapers and Magazines for Kids

TIME for Kids—A Time Life Magazine for Kids

http://www.timeforkids.com/TFK/

This is the online version of the popular news magazine for children. Its many sections include News, Sports, Entertainment, Who's News, Kid Reporters' Articles, Homework Helper, and Games and Trivia.

Kid's Castle—Smithsonian Magazine for Kids

http://www.kidscastle.si.edu/

At this online magazine from the Smithsonian, students can read articles, look at pictures, and post messages about people and topics in sports, history, science, art, dance, travel, nature and wildlife, and people and culture.

World Magazine from National Geographic

http://www.nationalgeographic.com/ngkids/

World Magazine has been designed to entertain and educate kids ages 6 to 14. It is an interactive multitopic magazine and online site that focuses on the subjects of interest to kids—animals, entertainment, science, technology, current events, and cultures from around the world. It has great stories, games, and interactive projects.

National Geographic Explorer

http://magma.nationalgeographic.com/ngexplorer/

This site has wonderful activities for both younger children and older children. It is bright and engaging, with lots to explore, such as their polling booth that asks for students' opinions. They also have stories, games, challenges, and e-cards for all to enjoy. Their Kids Stuff section has Bookmarks, Cartoons, Coloring Books, Creature Feature, Homework Help, Kids News, Map Machine, and National Geographic Kids. It is a fun and exciting site for kids.

Online Reference Sites for Teachers and Students [cont.]

Newspapers and Magazines for Kids [cont.]

Scholastic News

http://teacher.scholastic.com/scholasticnews/index.asp

The Scholastic News site has News, Special Reports, Kids Press Corps, Vote Now, Games and Quizzes, Movies, TV and Music, and Sports sections. It also has a wonderful Homework Hub with a search tool to help students find the help they need. It includes an Organize, Research, Practice, Write, and Prepare section, an Every Day Essential section, and a Tip of the Week section.

Odyssey Adventures in Science Magazine

http://www.odysseymagazine.com/

This science magazine is for kids, ages 10–16. Kids can explore this site for the latest news in science, and they can check out special science features just for kids such as Star Gazing with Jack Horkheimer, Ask a Scientist, live Webcams, and Mystery Photos.

Yes Magazine

http://www.yesmag.bc.ca/

This is Canada's science magazine for kids. There are Brain Bumpers, Feature Stories, a Make Your Own Project section, and Bug Beat. The many at-home projects are interesting and well designed to make them easy for kids to use.

Sports Illustrated for Kids

http://www.sikids.com/

This site is great for the sports enthusiasts. It features news, games, e-cards, fantasy sports, and sports videos.

Weekly Reader

http://www.weeklyreader.com/

This is the website for the *Weekly Reader* educational magazine. While many classrooms subscribe to this magazine for their students, its website is a great place to visit, too. It has a kid's section with contests, games and activities, a teen section with a blog, contests and games, a teacher section with downloads, resources, and other classroom-related materials.

Online References

Online Reference Sites for Teachers and Students [cont.]

Newspapers and Magazines for Kids [cont.]

Stone Soup

http://www.stonesoup.com/

Stone Soup's online site is a great place for students to go who would like to read what other students have written and would like to submit writing of their own to websites that accept student writing. They have reading, writing, and art sections, plus links for young writers.

Highlights Magazine

http://www.highlightskids.com/

This is a wonderful site for young students. It has an animated Hidden Picture section, a Fun Finder section, a Games and Giggles Section, an Express Yourself section, a Story Soup section, and a Science in Action section. Students will enjoy exploring the activities at this site.

Owl Kids Online

http://www.owlkids.com/

This is the online home of *Chirp*, *ChickaDEE*, and *Owl* magazines for children. It includes games, puzzles, coloring pages, current events, and activities geared to each age group.

Cricket Magazine Online

http://www.cricketmag.com/kids_home.asp

Cricket Magazine publishes *Babybug*, *Ladybug*, *Click*, *Spider*, *Ask*, *Cricket*, *Muse*, and *Cicada*—educational magazines for kids from 6 months through the teen years. They have material to read, activities, games, and contests at their online site.

Boy's Life

http://www.boyslife.org/

Boy's Life is connected to the *Boys' Life Magazine* and the Boy Scout organization. It offers activities, workshop ideas, games, jokes, skills to learn, a code master to make codes, contests, and opportunities to earn badges. If any of your students are involved in scouting, be sure to pass on this address on to them.

Online References

Online Reference Sites for Teachers and Students [cont.]

Online Grammar, Punctuation, and Spelling Help

A Guide to Grammar and Writing

http://grammar.ccc.commnet.edu/grammar/

Capital Community College Foundation sponsors this Guide to Grammar and Writing. This site offers guides for writing at the word and sentence level, the paragraph level, and the essay and research paper level. It also has an Ask Grammar Question section, a Quizzes section, and a Search Devices section. There are several *PowerPoint* presentations available to help students understand important rules of grammar and writing. This is an excellent site, one that should be bookmarked by your students for continual reference use.

Principles of Composition

http://grammar.ccc.commnet.edu/grammar/composition/composition.htm

The Capital Community College Foundation also sponsors this site. It contains sections called The Writing Process, Structural Considerations, and Patterns of Composition. This site should also be bookmarked by your students for continual reference use.

Grammar Helper

http://www.kidinfo.com/Language_Arts/Grammar_Helper.html

This site has many resources for students and teachers to use. Its sections include Capitalization, Grammar Guides, Linguistics Fun, Punctuation, Spelling, and Vocabulary Building. The sites provided are interactive and engaging for students and can provide motivation for them to work on their skills. The Spelling section for example includes:

Spell Check: An interactive spelling challenge to practice spelling words with different levels of difficulty

SpellaRoo: A spelling game

Spelling It Right: Printable spelling exercise worksheets

National Spelling Bee: Information about the National Spelling Bee with study tips and lesson plans for teachers

SpellWeb: Students can enter a word the way they think it is spelled to check if it is the correct spelling. If it is not, the correct spelling will be provided.

Online Reference Sites for Teachers and Students [cont.]

Writing Format and Style Guides

APA Style—Formatting and Style Guide

http://www.apastyle.org

This is the home page for the American Psychological Association Style site. Their editorial style details the style for punctuation and abbreviations, the construction of tables, the selection of headings, presentation of statistics, and the citation of references. Most schools are primarily concerned with the citation of references. Check out this site for tips and links to purchasing books published by APA.

APA Formatting and Style Guide

http://owl.english.purdue.edu/owl/resource/560/01/

The American Psychological Association style is most commonly used to cite sources within the social sciences. This resource offers examples for the general format of APA research papers, in-text citations, endnotes/footnotes, and the reference page. Purdue University's site, The Owl at Purdue—Free Writing Help and Teaching Resources, also provides APA style and citation help.

MLA Writing Formatting and Style Guide

http://www.mla.org/style

This is the home page for the Modern Language Association (MLA) writing style. It is the other most commonly used writing style. They do not publish their style guidelines on the Web, but their hard copy publications can be ordered at this site.

MLA Writing Style and Citation

http://owl.english.purdue.edu/owl/resource/557/01/

The MLA writing style and citation rules are concerned with the mechanics of writing, such as punctuation, quotation, and documentation and citation of sources. Purdue University's site, The Owl at Purdue—Free Writing Help and Teaching Resources, provides MLA style and citation help as well as guides to the writing process. Their guides include The Writing Process, Professional, Technical, and Scientific Writing, Job Search Writing, General Academic Writing, Research and Citation, Grammar and Mechanics, English as a Second Language (ESL), Literary Analysis and Criticism, Writing in the Social Sciences, Writing in Engineering, Creative Writing, Teaching Writing, and Tutoring Writing. This is an excellent site with step-by-step directions to help your students write better.

Online References

Technology Resources

Introduction

There are many things to know about using and teaching technology. This section is organized with several different perspectives in mind. The government agencies section provides the sites that have the resources teachers need to be able to review the role that federal and state governments play in determining our technology programs.

Other sites have been provided to help educators learn how computers, the Internet, peripheral devices, and other electronics works. Some sites offer explanations, while others offer tutorials and activities that teachers or students can use.

There is also a section with WebQuests. A WebQuest is an inquiry-oriented activity in which most or all of the information used by learners comes from the Web. WebQuests are designed to use learners' time well, to focus on using information rather than looking for it, and to support learners' thinking at the higher levels of analysis, synthesis, and evaluation.

Internet safety is of utmost importance. Educators, parents, and students must know what to do to keep everyone safe. These sites offer opportunities to visit some of the best Web-safety resources available.

SUGGESTED activity

Have your students use the sites in this section to find the answers to relevant computer operation questions. Then, have your students make up reference cards titled "All I ever wanted to know about…" to use as a resource in your classroom. Students might also want to try making a *PowerPoint* presentation or some other multimedia project to share what they know about a particular computer system or other "How Computers Work" topics.

Technology

Computer Magazines

Technology and Learning Magazine

http://www.techlearning.com/

The Technology and Learning Network is the home of the *Technology and Learning Magazine*. It provides administrators, technology professionals, and teachers with comprehensive information on technology trends, new products, news, and funding sources for their technology programs. TechLearning.com offers a free subscription *Technology and Learning Magazine* and the Technology and Learning Newsletter. Be sure your school receives this excellent magazine.

T.H.E. Journal

http://thejournal.com/

T.H.E. Journal is dedicated to improve and advance technology within districts, schools, and classrooms. Launched in 1972, T.H.E. Journal was the first magazine to cover education technology. T.H.E. Journal has a monthly magazine, two websites—thejournal.com and EduHound.com—and four newsletters—K–12 Tech Trends, T.H.E. SmartClassroom, EduHound Weekly, and T.H.E. Focus. You should visit this site and make sure your school receives its publications.

Connected Newsletter

http://corporate.classroom.com/newsletter.html

This subscription newsletter is a great resource for technology integration. First published in 1994, the *Connected Newsletter* remains a practical and popular resource that helps teachers incorporate technology and the Internet into their teaching. Look at their sample pages or try a free trial. Published nine times a year, each issue of the *Connected Newsletter* includes articles, useful tips, and countless website resources that teachers can choose from depending on what they are teaching in the classroom that day.

ZDNET—Technology News

http://www.zdnet.com/

Use ZDNET to find out the latest in technology and electronics. They report on technology equipment testing and product reviews, offer free and safe downloads, provide online learning opportunities, and give price comparisons. This is an excellent site to use when students are learning about technology equipment and how to purchase it.

Technology Resources [cont.]

Computer Magazines [cont.]

PC Magazine

http://www.pcmag.com/

PC Magazine provides comprehensive product evaluations based on benchmark tests from PC Magazine Labs. They also feature people in the PC industry, and provide in-depth reports on the latest technologies.

Computer User

http://www.computeruser.com/

Computer User offers daily computer articles along with news, reviews, computer dictionary, ISP search, training directory, and resources.

Computerworld Magazine

http://www.computerworld.com/

This magazine is an information source for information about laptops, desktops, software, hardware, security provisions, networking, and storage.

Mac Life

http://www.maclife.com/

Mac Life is a monthly magazine for the Macintosh computer user.

MacWorld

http://www.macworld.com

MacWorld features practical how-tos, in-depth features, the latest troubleshooting tips and tricks, industry news, future trends, and much more. This is an important resource for the schools and classrooms that use Mac technology.

Technology

Technology Resources (cont.)

Education Resources

The Apple Learning Interchange (ALI)

http://edcommunity.apple.com/ali/

The Apple Learning Interchange (ALI) is a network for educators. It offers content ranging from simple lesson ideas to in-depth curriculum units for K–12 educators and higher education faculty. It provides campus projects, research, and more. You can create your own free account and gain access to publishing and collaboration resources with movies, images, and sounds. Other resources include information about Apple products and events, a description of Apple classrooms of tomorrow, and results of research on the effect of technology on teaching and learning. This site has much to offer both Mac and PC users.

Microsoft Education

http://www.microsoft.com/education/default.mspx

Working closely with education communities, Microsoft has developed technology, tools, programs, and solutions to help address education challenges while improving teaching and learning opportunities. Microsoft hopes that educators find new ways to enhance student learning through technology. You can learn how to use and integrate Microsoft software in your classroom. They offer in-depth step-by-step tutorials and tips and tricks. You can also view lesson plans from Microsoft by subject area for grades K–12. This site is an excellent resource to use if you would like to learn more about using Microsoft software.

Global SchoolNet Foundation—Global Schoolhouse

http://www.globalschoolnet.org/GSH/

Global Schoolhouse is the original virtual meeting place where educators, students, parents, and community members can collaborate. It combines teaching ideas, Web publishing, video conferencing, and other online tools so that students around the world can participate in project-based online learning activities. Since it began, Global SchoolNet has connected more than a million students from 45,000 schools in 194 countries. Recently, President George W. Bush joined Global SchoolNet Director Yvonne Andres and leaders of other organizations to form Friendship through Education, a group that will connect U.S. students and students in countries with Muslim populations in a curriculum-based project. Check all the projects at Global SchoolNet to see if any of them suit your students' needs.

Technology Resources (cont.)

Education Resources (cont.)

Education World—School Notes

http://www.schoolnotes.com/edgate/enter.php

School Notes is a free community service from Education World that provides teachers the opportunity to create notes for homework and class information and post them on the web. Students and their parents can view these notes by entering their school's zip code. School Notes is so easy that you can learn how to use it in seconds. To start a School Notes account, check out this address: **http://www.schoolnotes.com/edgate/usersguide.php**.

Education World—Interactivity Center

http://www.education-world.com/a_tech/archives/interactivity.shtml

This site is exciting and engaging. There are so many interactive projects for kids of all ages. The site features collaborative projects, virtual field trips, educational games, and other interactive activities. Some activities are ongoing while others have specific schedules.

Education World—Tech Lessons of the Week Archive

http://www.education-world.com/a_tech/archives/techlp.shtml

This is the spot to visit for more great technology lessons. There are so many different types of lessons. There is something special here for every student, teacher, and classroom. There is also a great graphic listing of many of the other technology opportunities available at this site. Be sure to visit this site. You will definitely be able to find something you can use right away with your class.

Education World—EdTech Tips of the Week

http://www.education-world.com/a_tech/archives/tech_tips.shtml

There are so many technology-related problems that classroom and technology teachers face. We all need simple solutions so we do not panic when problems occur. The problem-solving tips presented here are in an easy-to-understand format.

Education Resources [cont.]

Discovery School—Technology Lesson Plans

http://school.discovery.com/lessonplans/tech.html

There are many technology lesson plans at Discovery School. They are grouped by grade levels—Grades K–5, Grades 6–8, and Grades 9–12. Each lesson plan includes everything you need—objectives, materials, procedure, adaptations, discussion questions, evaluation, extensions, suggested reading, links, vocabulary, and standards.

NETS for Teachers

http://www.iste.org/inhouse/nets/cnets/teachers/index.html

National Educational Technology Standards for Teachers (NETS) is an excellent resource for teachers to review. Sample lesson plans with the standards and performance indicators, as well as rubrics for scoring students, make this a very robust site.

Government Agencies

Office of Educational Technology (OET)

http://www.ed.gov/about/offices/list/os/technology/index.html

The Office of Educational Technology is responsible for coordinating the development and implementation of the Department's educational technology policies, research projects, and national technology summits. In 2005, OET produced The National Education Technology Plan, which provides a summary of the challenges in our schools, the importance of technology, current student attitudes regarding technology, and recommendations for meeting the challenges of No Child Left Behind through technology. Review the details of this report and check out additional student, teacher, administrator, and parent resources.

Regional Technology in Education Consortia (RTEC)—Resource Center

http://www.rtec.org/

For 10 years, the U.S. Department of Education funded a nationwide initiative called the Regional Technology in Education Consortia (RTEC). While funding changed somewhat in 2005, this site still provides excellent programs and resources. The resource categories at this site include planning and evaluation, professional development, teacher and learning, grade-level resources, integrating technology, technology highlights, and special topics resources.

Technology

Technology Resources

How Computers Work

How Stuff Works

http://computer.howstuffworks.com/

How Stuff Works is a great place to go if you want to know how something works or you need an answer to a technology question. This site offers thorough but simple explanations that are easy to understand. Whether your question is something like "Does adding more RAM to your computer make it faster?" or "How can a Windows virus end up on an iPod?" this is the site to use.

Education World—Techtorials

http://www.education-world.com/a_tech/archives/techtorials.shtml

Techtorials can make all the difference between being uncomfortable or comfortable with a computer skill. This site offers easy-to-follow tutorials on the following topics: computer basics, computer maintenance and trouble shooting, the Internet, Web design, email, *Office*, *Word*, *PowerPoint*, *Excel*, Apple hardware and software, keyboarding, professional development, and curriculum and emerging technologies. Try one of these Techtorials to see if you find the process helpful.

Fact Monsters—Computers and Technology

http://www.factmonster.com/ipka/A0772279.html

Fact Monsters—Computers and Technology is a database with topics like How Do Computers Work? Computer Glossary, Computer Virus Time Line, How Big Is a Bit?, Internet Safety Guide, Internet Time Line, and many more. This is a great place for students to learn more about computers and technology.

Answers that Work—The Home of Practical Computing

http://www.answersthatwork.com/library.htm

In the Answers that Work Library, you can find help to fix computer problems, fix computer errors, or tune up your PC. Some of the topics include software answers and PC tips, hardware problems, configuration solutions, networking tips, general computer tips, recommendations, drivers, software downloads, task list, PC tune-up, and PC performance. This site offers very specialized help and information. Look up your computer model to get the help you need.

Technology

Technology Resources (cont.)

How Computers Work (cont.)

Click and Learn—What's Inside a Computer

http://www.kids-online.net/learn/c_n_l.html

All you or your students need to do to begin to learn about the inside of a computer is to select the present skill level—Master, Junior, or Novice. Then, just click on different computer parts to learn about them. This is a great interactive visual-based learning resource.

Intel Education—The Journey Inside

http://www.intel.com/education/journey/

The Journey Inside is a collection of 35 interactive online lessons for students to complete. This curriculum is divided into six sections: Introduction to Computers, Circuits and Switches, Digital Information, Microprocessors, The Internet, and Technology and Society. This interactive resource uses interactive Flash activities, virtual field trips, audio, and other activities to guide students to a better understanding of the world of technology. Your students can work on these lessons from the classroom, during free moments, or even from home.

3D Computer Term Dictionary

http://www.maran.com/dictionary/index.html

This dictionary provides simple definitions for hundreds of computer technology-based terms. Graphic illustrations are also included to add to comprehension of the words.

How Computers Work WebQuest

http://www.tim-jansen.com/lessons_misc/how_computers_work_webquest/index.htm

This WebQuest project requires students to complete several small projects over the course of a number of classes. Depending on their grade level and expertise, they have different assignments to complete. Some of the topics include creating a "How Computers Work" booklet or a computer dictionary, identifying and describing various parts of a computer, writing an essay on computer viruses, or writing a paper on the history of computers.

Technology Resources [cont.]

Internet Safety

Surf Swell

http://disney.go.com/surfswell/index.html

The Surf Swell Island site is an adventure game. Internet safety material is presented using a series of three games, each featuring a classic Disney character, and focusing on an area of concern: privacy, viruses, or netiquette. A mini quiz follows each of the three games to reinforce what was presented. The exciting Challenge of Doom mega quiz brings together the content from all three games. Answering correctly gives children access to a collection of fun Surf Swell-themed activities located in a password-protected Treasure Palace. This is a fun place to go to help young students understand some of the safety issues involved with using the Internet.

Safekids.Com

http://www.safekids.com

Safe Kids Tips and Tools is a guide to making the Internet safe, fun, and productive. While this site was designed for parents, it is an excellent resource for the classroom too. Its topic sections include Child Safety on the Information Highway, Video and Audio Slide Shows, Kids Rules for Online Safety, Chat Room Safety and Privacy Issues, Guidelines for Parents, and a Family Contract for Online Safety. All these topics are important to review with your students and their families.

SafeTeens

http://www.safeteens.com/

This is a companion site to Safekids. It too, is a guide to making the Internet safe, fun, and productive. Some of its topics include Teen Guide to Safe Blogging, Safe Blogging Tips for Teens, How to Recognize Grooming, Teen Safety on the Information Highway, Guidelines for Parents of Teens, Protect your Privacy, Internet Acronyms Every Parent Needs to Know from NetLingo, and Timely Articles and Blog Entries.

iSafe

http://www.isafe.org/

Founded in 1998, i-SAFE Inc. has become the leader in Internet Safety Education. I-SAFE is a nonprofit foundation whose mission is to educate and empower youth to make their Internet experiences safe and responsible. They want to educate students on how to avoid dangerous, inappropriate, or unlawful online behavior on the Internet. I-SAFE accomplishes this through a K–12 curriculum, and community outreach programs for parents, law enforcement, and community leaders.

Technology

Internet Safety [cont.]

WiredKids

http://www.wiredkids.org/

A large portion of Wired Kids, Inc.'s work involves preventing and helping investigate cybercrimes and abuses. WiredKids.org also has online safety games for younger children, information for children of all ages, and helpful information for teachers, parents, and law enforcement.

FBI Publication: A Parents Guide to Internet Safety

http://www.fbi.gov/publications/pguide/pguidee.htm

The FBI suggests that one of the most important factors in keeping children safe online is using appropriate blocking software and parental controls. They also stress the importance of open, honest discussions with children, monitoring online activity, and following the tips in their *A Parents Guide to Internet Safety* pamphlet. Review this site, and then if you feel it is appropriate, share it with your students' parents. Also, have your students visit the FBI: Kids' Page.

FBI: Kids' Page

http://www.fbi.gov/fbikids.htm

The Kids' Page is designed for children and their parents to learn more about the FBI through age-appropriate games, tips, stories, and interactives. They will also introduce your students to their working dogs and show how FBI special agents and analysts investigate cases. This site is a good follow-up to discussions about crime on the Internet.

Yahoo, Safety on the Internet—A Fun Guide to Internet Safety

http://safely.yahoo.com/

This is a fun, interactive site that helps students understand some of the issues surrounding Internet safety. It includes games and activities, clips and videos, a Teen Speak section, and an In the Know section. There is also a section for parents that includes Parenting Online, Is Your Child at Risk?, Downloading Music, a Parents' Forum and a Get Involved section.

One of the best sections at Yahoo, Safety on the Internet is called Internet Safety 1-2-3 by Parry Aftab. He has devised three easy steps to learn about Internet safety. The steps he suggests are for parents, but they will work equally well in a classroom.

Technology

Technology Resources [cont.]

Internet Safety [cont.]

NetSmartz Workshop—Keeping Kids and Teens Safer on the Internet

http://www.netsmartz.org/

The NetSmartz Workshop is an interactive educational-safety resource from the National Center for Missing and Exploited Children and the Boys and Girls Clubs of America. It is intended for children ages 5 to 17, parents, guardians, educators, and law enforcement. It uses age-appropriate 3-D interactive games and activities to teach children how to stay safe on the Internet. It is bright and colorful, engaging, and very worthwhile. Share it with your students at school and have them share it with their parents at home.

iKeep Safe—The Internet Keep Safe Coalition

http://www.ikeepsafe.org/

Governors and first spouses formed The Internet Keep Safe Coalition in partnership with a crime-prevention organizations, law enforcement agencies, foundations, and corporate sponsors. Its goal is to teach the basic rules of Internet safety to children online and in schools.

iKeep Safe for Kids—Activities for Kids

http://www.ikeepsafe.org/iksc_kids/

This is the fun part of the iKeep Safe site. It has games, activities, and coloring story pages for kids to do.

iKeep Safe for Parents—Everything You Need to Keep Your Family Safe Online

http://www.ikeepsafe.org/PRC/

This is a great parent resource center with activities, lessons, and videos. There is also iKeep Safe Parents, a moderated Yahoo Group for parents, grandparents, and others who are concerned about online child safety and safe usage of technology by young people.

iKeep Safe—For Educators—Presentations and Training Materials

http://www.ikeepsafe.org/iksc_educators/

From iKeep Safe, the Faux Paw presentations and training materials are available for download at no cost for teaching Internet safety in group educational settings.

Technology

Technology Resources (cont.)

Technology Organizations, Conferences, and Workshops

International Society for Technology in Education (ISTE)

http://www.iste.org/

The International Society for Technology in Education (ISTE) is the largest teacher-based nonprofit organization in the field of educational technology. It is a nonprofit membership organization that works to improve education by advancing the effective use of technology in Pre-K–12 and teacher education. It is the home of the National Educational Technology Standards (NETS), the Center for Applied Research in Educational Technology (CARET), and the National Educational Computing Conference (NECC). ISTE represents more than 85,000 professionals worldwide. They support their members with resources, information, and networking opportunities.

NECC—National Educational Computing Conference

http://web.uoregon.edu/ISTE/NECC2006/about_NECC/future_NECCs.php

For more than 20 years, National Educational Computing Conference has been the premier educational technology conference. This annual conference, presented by ISTE, includes hands-on workshops, lecture-format and interactive concurrent sessions, discussions with key industry leaders, and one of the largest educational technology exhibits in the world.

CUE—Computer-Using Educators

http://www.cue.org/

Computer-Using Educators, Inc. is a nonprofit California corporation founded in 1978. CUE's goal is to advance student achievement through technology in all disciplines from preschool through college. With an active current membership of thousands of educational professionals, CUE supports many regional affiliates and Special Interest Groups. CUE Conferences are California's premier educational technology events. CUE is the largest organization of its type in the West and one of the largest in the United States.

Technology

Technology Resources

Technology Organizations, Conferences, and Workshops (cont.)

Technology in Education

http://www.newhorizons.org/strategies/technology/front_tech.htm

Many people worry that computers will be used inappropriately in the classroom. This worry existed with the other "new" technologies like the radio and TV. There are opportunities out there, and this site will help you sort the good from the bad. At this site, you will find information about how computers can be used with students to stimulate and develop writing skills, collaborate with peers in foreign countries, do authentic research, and do complex kinds of problem solving that would otherwise be impossible. Their articles and resources can be used to develop a comprehensive technology plan. They also provide detailed information on design, wiring, equipment, and physical infrastructure modifications necessary for implementing technology within a school. This site is an excellent planning resource for teachers, schools, and districts.

Teacher Created Materials Publishing—Professional Development

http://www.teachercreatedmaterials.com/professionalDevelopment

Teacher Created Materials is a leader in providing professional development directly to schools. Whether you need a two-hour workshop or several full day sessions, they can customize a program for you. Their workshops cover many educational teaching and administrative topics. Some of their workshop titles include 101 Easy Ways to Use the Internet in Your Classroom or Lab, How to Use Simple Computer Activities in Your Classroom or Lab, Effective Teaching with Multiple Intelligences, How to Improve Your Students' Nonfiction Reading and Writing Skills, How to Successfully Implement Literacy Learning Centers, A Beginner's Guide to Creating School and Classroom Web Pages, and more. Be sure to check out what Teacher Created Materials Publishing has to offer and consider using their many resources.

WebQuests

WebQuest—San Diego State University

http://webquest.sdsu.edu/

This site was designed to serve as a resource for those who are using the WebQuest model to teach. The WebQuest model was developed in early in 1995 at San Diego State University by Bernie Dodge with Tom March and was outlined then in "Some Thoughts About WebQuests." Since then, instructors have made use of the resources on this site to offer scores of workshops to teachers. Since 1996, San Diego State University has maintained a database of examples of more than 2,500 WebQuests. This site is a great place to learn about WebQuests and find ones that will work with your curriculum in your classroom.

Technology

Technology Resources [cont.]

WebQuests [cont.]

Best WebQuests.com

http://bestwebquests.com/

This site focuses on helping teachers create the best possible WebQuests. The site is managed by Tom March—one of the educators who participated in the development of the WebQuest process. The site provides excellent links and resources with Portals, Online WebQuest Makers, WebQuest Design Guides, Articles, Training and Professional Development, and Learning Theory and Pedagogy.

Discovery School Com—Kathy Schrock—WebQuests

http://school.discovery.com/schrockguide/webquest/webquest.html

Kathy Schrock finds that Web Quests are a perfect model for teachers searching for ways to incorporate the Internet into the classroom on both a short-term and long-term basis. She provides a *PowerPoint* presentation based on the information found at Bernie Dodge's WebQuest's site. She has designed a sample WebQuest titled "The 1960s Museum" and provided many other references. Kathy Schrock's teacher resources are always worth reviewing and this one is no exception.

Test Practice and Homework Help

Introduction

One of the biggest pressures on students is to do well on standardized tests. Whether they are at the elementary level of their education, at the high school level trying to get into the best colleges, or at the college level trying to get into graduate school, today's world requires that students take these tests and be assessed by their performances on them. Studies show that preparation for standardized tests, particularly practice related directly to the kinds and format of the questions being asked, can make a significant difference in a student's results. Teachers should familiarize themselves with the tests students will need to take and the ways they can receive help online or in their local community.

Students need ways to practice what they are learning. Homework is often required by teachers to help students practice and reinforce the skills they are learning at school. Having good homework habits and the appropriate resources available to students is essential. The appropriate use of technology, computers, and the Internet can help students be successful in school and in their preparation for their lives after they finish school.

SUGGESTED activity

Have high school students look at the Test Prep Review site at **http://www.testprepreview.com/**. Have them look through the Test Preparation section to see what suggestions they make for doing well on tests. Make sure they focus on what activities would work for them so they could do their best. Have them explore specific test Web pages too. Visit Teacher Created Materials Publishing at **http://www.teachercreatedmaterials.com** and search for materials that might be relevant your students. The activities are standards based and titles relate to specific skills. Two examples are *Standards-Based Comprehension Strategies and Skills Practice Book*, and *Writing Preparation for the SAT*. Each publication provides free downloadable sample pages, the table of contents for the material, and the related standards and grant money that may be available to teachers or schools to purchase the materials. This type of search for materials is always worth the time.

Test Practice and Homework Help [cont.]

General

Test Prep Review

http://www.testprepreview.com/

This site offers a review of the top test-taking sites and free practice tests. This is a great site to begin with when you are checking into required tests for private schools, high schools, colleges, and professional college programs like law or business. This exceptional site should be shared with students and parents.

Internet 4 Classrooms—Assessment

http://www.internet4classrooms.com/assistance.htm

This site provides a variety of resources to help students practice skills required on various assessments. They have divided their resources into elementary, middle school and high school level tests. They also provide a countdown timer that can be of benefit to some students.

The New York Times—Who's Who and What's What Quiz

http://www.nytimes.com/learning/students/quiz/index.html

Have your students see what they know about the day's news. The daily quiz provides questions and images that relate to articles published in *The New York Times* each day. Students can play every Monday through Friday. This is a great way to keep students interested in studying what is happening in the world on a daily basis. The site also includes News Summaries, Daily News Quizzes, Word of the Day, Test Prep Question of the Day, Science Question and Answer, Letters to the Editor, and Ask a Reporter.

High School Ace: The Academic Homepage for High School Students

http://highschoolace.com/ace/ace.cfm

The Academic Homepage for High School Students is a site that will help students prepare for their college-prep exams and standardized tests. If students visit this site each day and participate in the test-taking prep activities, they will benefit from the professional help available at this site as they work on their skills. This site offers high school homework help and college-prep study guides to students in the areas of English, foreign languages, math, science, U.S. history, and world history. They also have a College Guide, Daily News Quiz, Test Prep Question, Today's News, Weather Forecast, and a Word of the Day section.

Test Practice and Homework Help (cont.)

Homework Help

Homework Spot

http://www.homeworkspot.com/

HomeworkSpot.com is a free homework information site that features the some useful K–12 homework-related sites. With the help of students, parents, and teachers, their team of educators, librarians, and journalists has collected the best resources for English, math, science, history, art, music, technology, foreign language, college prep, health, life skills, extracurricular activities, and much more. They have organized these resources into grade-appropriate categories with access to many of the world's best libraries, museums, and current event sources. Because no homework is complete without a study break, they have also included a wide assortment of fun mind-stretching activities and contests for students to enjoy. This is a great site for your students to use.

BJ Pinchbeck's Homework Help

http://school.discovery.com/homeworkhelp/bjpinchbeck/

BJ Pinchbeck's Homework Help from The Discovery Channel School is for anyone who needs help with homework. "If you can't find it here, then you just can't find it" is the promise on the site's header. The homework links at this site include Art/Music, Computer Science and the Internet, English, Foreign Languages, Health and P.E., Math, News, Recess, Reference, Science, Search Engines, and Social Studies. This is a great site for your students to bookmark or add to their favorites list.

Study Buddy

http://homework-help.aol.com/

This is a search engine specifically developed by AOL for homework help. Students can search by subject area or enter a question into Study Buddy search and find the homework answers they need. StudyBuddy.com searches many content databases and thousands of educator-approved websites. Study Buddy presents results in these categories: Best Results, Articles, Audio and Video, Photos/Maps, Quizzes/Games, Web Sites, and Family Library. Students can also choose their grade level and browse through thousands of articles on hundreds of topics, all designed to help with their homework. Study Buddy also has a dictionary, thesaurus, atlas, and a translator. Students can also test their U.S. IQ by taking the American Quest for grades 3–5 or 6–8.

Test Practice and Homework Help (cont.)

Homework Help (cont.)

Jiskha Homework Help

http://www.jiskha.com/

At Jiskha Homework Help, more than 200 experts volunteer their time to assist students. More than 4,000 students receive personal help with homework every day. Students can look for help by jumping to different curriculum-related sections or they can search the site for specific help. There are literally thousands of educational articles that are used for guidance and support of students with troublesome assignments.

Reference Desk—Homework Help

http://www.refdesk.com/

http://www.refdesk.com/homework.html

The Reference Desk site and its subsection, Homework, are a bit busy looking in appearance but they offer a wealth of information. It is well worth exploring to see what these two sites have to offer your students. Students may need some guided assistance with navigating this site to see its full potential.

TIME for Kids Homework Helper

http://www.timeforkids.com/TFK/hh

TIME for Kids has a kid-powered Rapid Research Tool that helps direct students to the best sites on the Web by using subject selection. They also have a Write Ideas and a Go Places section that can be of help to students too.

Discoveryschool—Homework Helper and More

http://school.discovery.com/students/

Discovery Channel offers Cosmeo, a fast and fun online homework-help service. Besides homework help, Cosmeo offers reliable report information, math help, and brain games.

Science Fair Central

http://school.discovery.com/Sciencefaircentral/

This site provides students, teacher, and parents with a comprehensive guide to creating a science-fair project.

Test Practice and Homework Help (cont.)

Homework Help (cont.)

Kid Info—Student Homework Help

http://www.kidinfo.com/School_Subjects.html

This site offers homework help in the basic subject areas, plus links to search engines, reference resources, and fun sites to try when the homework is done.

First Gov for Kids—Homework Help

http://www.kids.gov/k_homework.htm

This site opens with "Confused by a computer question? Stumped on a science question? Heartburn over a history question? Here are some great links to help you with your homework—this may even help you finish it faster!" This site has many links to homework related websites. Students should explore this site, to see what it has to offer.

Teacher-Generated Worksheets and Study Guides

Half-Baked Software

http://hotpot.uvic.ca/

The Hot Potatoes software suite at this site includes six applications, enabling you to create interactive multiple-choice, short-answer, jumbled-sentence, crossword, matching/ordering, and gap-fill exercises for the Web. Hot Potatoes is not freeware, but it is free of charge for those working for publicly funded nonprofit educational institutions that make their pages available on the Web. If you are making a class Web page, try this software to make your Web page more interactive.

Personal Educational Press

http://www.educationalpress.org/

At this site, you can create free educational test practice aids such as flashcards, game boards, study sheets, and quizzes for your students. After you create your materials, they can be printed directly from your browser. You can use words and definitions that have been provided for specific educational curriculum content areas, or you can insert your own material to make the practice aids relevant to what needs to be studied or reviewed in your class.

Test Practice and Homework Help [cont.]

Teacher-Generated Worksheets and Study Guides [cont.]

RHL School

http://www.rhlschool.com/

RHL School has hundreds of free worksheets for teachers and parents to copy for their children. They have worksheets for English basics, mathematics, reading comprehension, and reference skills. You can print these worksheets right from your Web browser.

Homeschooling Adventures—Worksheets

http://www.homeschoolingadventures.com/worksheets.html

A homeschooling mom created this site. There is more to this site than the worksheet section, but this section is worth a look. It has a listing of online sites with free worksheets, as well as software to help you create your own!

TLS Books.com—Worksheets

http://www.tlsbooks.com

This site offers worksheets for classroom use for the following categories: preschool, kindergarten, first grade, second grade, third grade, fourth grade, fifth grade, multigrade, spelling, holidays, math, English, geography, history, and science. Look to see if there are resources here that you can use with your class.

#50475—*Must-See Websites for Busy Teachers*